TOP-DOWN INNOVATION

Create an Innovative Company!

BOTTOM-UP INNOVATION

Innovate your Way to Success!

Joseph N. Stein

SI Publishing

TOP-DOWN INNOVATION
BOTTOM-UP INNOVATION

This material and the information contained in it is the property of Simply Innovate™. No part of this document or the related information may be reproduced or transmitted in any form, by any means (electronic, photocopying, recording, or otherwise) without the prior written permission of Simply Innovate™. All Rights Reserved.

Simply Innovate
30025 Alicia Parkway
Laguna Niguel, CA 92677
generalinfo@simplyinnovate.net

First Edition
ISBN # 978-0-9849224-3-7

Limits of Liability/Disclaimer of Warranty: While the author has used his best efforts in preparing this guide, he makes no representations or warranties with respect to the accuracy or completeness of the contents of this guide and specifically disclaims any implied warranties of merchantability or fitness for a particular purpose. No warranty may be created or extended by sales representatives or written sales materials. The advice and strategies contained herein may not be suitable for your situation. You should consult with other professionals where appropriate. The author shall not be liable for any loss of profit or any other commercial damages, not limited to special, incidental, consequential, or other damages.

Acknowledgements

Starting something new is exciting and scary, and I want to thank all the people who have taken some of the uncertainty away by giving me great advice and helping me along the my writing path. I am blessed to have talented and giving friends who are great sounding boards and advisors, key among them Patsy Estis, Mike Simmons, and Trudie Mitschang. Jack Eadon (and his wife Karen) and Maureen Aplin are established authors and also friends who helped me navigate the mysterious world of writing. I was so lucky to get introduced to some special people; my editor Ronale Rhodes, who has the detail eye that I sorely lack; Jeniffer, Anna and Julio over at Monkey Media, who created the fantastic book cover, and Scott over at Highly Trained Eye that helped with the interior book design. Special thanks go to my mentor and friend Steve Carley, who took time from his incredibly busy schedule to read and critique this book. Steve and the great folks over at the private equity firms Trimaran Capital Partners and Freeman Spogli were, perhaps unwittingly, a key factor in the writing of this book as they had the vision to see the value of innovation and allowed me to assume the SVP of Strategy & Innovation role at one of their companies, which is where my passion for innovation grew. Finally, I have to thank my lovely wife Cheryl who supports me in some many ways every day as I embark on my entrepreneurial endeavor and who provided me with some much-needed support with her detailed eye and her artistic direction.

Rich
you are my
strategic idol !
Joe St

What To Expect in These Books

If you are serious about innovation — not just reading about it, but actually innovating — then these books are for you. I can steer you to many other books that focus on creativity. I also can share with you an extensive list of entertaining books that have story after story about innovative companies and their successes (in fact, go to the Helpful Resources section of www.simplyinnovate.net to find them). In *Bottom-Up Innovation* and *Top-Down Innovation*, the theory is left in the shadows because action takes center stage. Action summaries are included throughout the books to help you take the necessary steps to innovate and achieve success!

These books are designed to be easy-to-understand and easy-to-read, yet they have all the essential building blocks you need to identify, ideate, and solve a business challenge using innovation (*Bottom-Up Innovation*) or to put together all the elements of an innovation environment to help a company continue to grow and outpace its competitors (*Top-Down Innovation*).

Website References

For you E-book readers, if your E-book device is internet enabled, you should be able to click on the many links in this book and get an enjoyable interactive experience. If you have older E-book readers or have purchased the print version of this book, all the website references are included in the back of the book. Check them out when you have a chance.

Foreword and Backward (aka Up and Down)

It's funny how innovation works. I was about halfway done writing what I thought was my first book, which was focused on helping small businesses innovate. I was struggling to find a great name for this book, even though I had the chapters pretty much laid out. So I decided to take a break and instead write a short guide (sort of like a workbook) to help small business people quickly solve a challenge or problem they have. Very cool. My first product.

Yet, while I was writing the book for employees in small businesses, I knew I also wanted to provide employees in mid-sized to large companies with a guide that explains how to innovate. This was special to me, since it is what I've spent most of my corporate life doing. But I was struggling with how to balance the information in the book to appeal to both executives and non-executives. After all, it is important to understand the challenges executives face when creating an innovation culture. But, most employees are not executives. Moreover, these employees may not work in an innovative company, but they may want to benefit from innovation.

This challenge was sitting in the back of my mind, and I was at a friend's house enjoying a late-summer celebrate-because-the-kids-are-going-back–to-school party, when someone called out for a toast and said: "Bottoms up!" That's all it took. It immediately struck me that this was a great description for employees trying to innovate in a non-innovative company. "Top-down" then popped into my brain. These words described where executives who want to create a lasting innovation environment need to start. I realized that these innovation concepts are really two separate discussions — and two separate books.

But I really liked the idea of putting both concepts in every reader's hands, because they are very complementary. That's how I ended up with this double-issue book.

If you are an employee who is not an executive or who does not exert significant influence over the direction of your company, start with *Bottom-up Innovation*.

Then, whether you work in a non-innovative or an innovative company, I recommend you read *Top-Down Innovation* (although it is optional). If you work in a non-innovative company, you will benefit from understanding what steps executives need to take to create a truly innovative company. And, in a future career, you may recognize those innovative characteristics, and you will have a leg up if your company ever decides to become more innovative. On the other hand, if you work in an innovative company, you may find some things your company can do better and, perhaps, influence the introduction of some improvements.

If you are an executive or a person of significant influence in your company, then *Top-Down Innovation* is written for you. After you are done, *Bottom-Up Innovation* is a must read, as it describes in detail the process of innovating that is not fully explained in *Top-Down Innovation*. It also gives you a perspective of what the employees charged with innovating are experiencing.

Happy reading!

BOTTOM-UP
INNOVATION

INNOVATE YOUR WAY TO SUCCESS!

Table of Contents – Bottom-Up Innovation

PART 1 – THE SET UP

Innovation is difficult when you work for a company that is not known for being innovative. It's even more difficult when you aren't one of the executives who have a say in the strategic direction of the company and how it operates. It's really, really difficult when your company has a wall of shame dedicated to photos of employees who were fired because they made a mistake.

The whole premise of *Bottom-Up Innovation* is based on the assumption that you work for a company that falls into one of the following categories:

➢ Absolutely does not embrace innovation
➢ Talks the talk about innovation but does little to promote and support innovation
➢ Really wants to innovate, but doesn't really know what to do (give an executive this book and tell him or her to read *Top-Down Innovation*)
☺ Has an elite innovation-killer squad that seeks out and destroys creativity, entrepreneurship, and free thinking in every nook and cranny of your company (since innovation should be fun, you'll see some humorous bullet points added from time to time)

The first three chapters of this book explore each of these company types to give you the ammunition you need to start innovating within the constraints of a non-innovative business environment.

If your company is really trying to be innovative and does support the birth of new ideas, Chapter 1 isn't as critical to you as someone who works in a company that is not innovative. Sorry, you still can't skip the chapter as it contains information pertinent to the rest of the book.

Chapters 2 and 3 are relevant, no matter what type of company you work for. Even the most innovative companies have managers and employees who live in the dark world of mediocrity and who lack the desire and character to support innovation. These chapters will help you spot these creativity-killers and will show you the obstructions they throw out in front of you as you are speeding down the innovation highway.

Chapter 1: Why Should I Care About Innovation Since My Company Doesn't?

Let's start with a little quiz. For each group of answers, select the one that best fits you:

A. I want to find ways to make my job easier.
B. Sure, I would like my job to be easier, but it's not my responsibility to try to change it.

A. I would like to get promoted so I can make more money.
B. I don't really like too much responsibility, so I am happy with my current job.

A. Sometimes I have difficulty getting the projects I'm in charge of completed on time and with successful results.
B. I really am not in charge of projects.

A. I see opportunities to do things better, but I don't know the best way to implement change.
B. I'm an "if it ain't broke, don't fix it" kind of person.

A. I like to learn new things.
B. I've already got enough stuff to deal with; I don't need to learn anything new right now.

A. I'm in sales, and I would like to increase my business.
B. I'm happy with the sales I'm bringing in.

A. I'm in charge of a department or business line for my company, and I would like to do one of the following: increase sales, reduce costs, improve a process, develop (or improve) a new product or service, or solve some other business challenge.
B. Yes, I'm in charge, and everything is running smoothly; no changes are necessary.

The great thing about the world and all seven-plus billion people in it is that we are all so different. I am awed by scientists who create computer components that are thousands of times smaller than the width of a human hair, or who create a supercollider that can smash protons together at nearly the speed of light. I could never do that. But, then again, maybe not everyone gets all excited about innovation like I do.

This book is not for everyone, but if you picked it up, chances are that you're not a complacent type of person; you're not content to watch life just pass you by. If you answered A to any of the questions above, this book will be valuable to you. We are going to have some fun and do some innovating over the next few pages and chapters.

I want to thank you for spending a little time with me; in return, I promise to make this book light on theory and heavy on action. As you know, this is really two books in one. The book you are reading, *Bottom-Up Innovation*, is geared toward anyone who works in a company, but is *not* one of the higher-level executives who can influence the strategic direction of the company. This book will help you whether your position is at the bottom of the "totem pole" or if you are a senior manager or department head. It also doesn't matter if you work for a small company or the biggest corporation.

The second book, *Top-Down Innovation*, is further back in these pages and is geared toward the higher-level executive who has the authority and control to make lasting changes in a company. Even small business owners would benefit from reading *Top-Down Innovation*, since they have that authority and control. If you don't fall into that category, I don't want to discourage you from reading *Top-Down Innovation*. There are some great insights into what a corporate leader needs to do to create lasting innovation. After all, you may be moving up the ladder someday soon, or you may decide to strike out and start your own business.

Let's spend a minute to make sure we are speaking the same language when it comes to innovation.

Innovation is: coming up with *and* implementing ideas that solve some sort of problem or challenge. Usually the reasons people innovate are to drive new sales, reduce costs, address competitive issues, improve a process, improve employee retention/involvement, or solve some other business challenge. I invite you to go to my website at www.simplyinnovate.net and click on the graphics on the home page (with the short videos that accompany them) that walk you through the four steps of innovation: identify, ideate, filter, and finish. It's a quick little overview in advance of some of the actionable details coming up in later chapters.

Now, you may hear different "innovation" terms thrown around like sustaining, incremental, substantial, significant, radical, disruptive, or breakthrough. It's true that some innovations are

more "Wow!" than others; after all, everyone knows that mp3 players killed CD players, which took out cassette tapes, which threw 8-track players under the bus, which made records obsolete. Those were all pretty disruptive changes. I know it was disruptive to me, because I spent a lot of money buying cassette tapes to replace those bulky 8-tracks I owned. (What, you don't know what an 8-track is? You must be under 30 years old.)

But fewer people think about how more incremental innovation — like Cascade detergent changing from powder to liquid to self-contained little pouches that combine powder with liquid cleaning agents — can benefit mankind and the companies that come up with these changes. These kinds of innovation are more common and are important because they can be very profitable.

Incremental Innovation

Once again, when people hear the word innovation, they tend to gravitate to new products, like the iPod. But innovation can come in the form of new processes or even a brand new business model. For instance, a seemingly minor innovation is being able to deposit checks in an ATM machine without using an envelope. But, while minor, this change saved banks millions of dollars in envelope costs and labor expenses, as well as increased customer satisfaction. (I love it because I don't have to fill out a deposit form, it's quicker and less work, and I get a scanned copy of the check on my receipt.) This innovation wasn't exciting or sexy, but it was innovative.

Bottom-Up Innovation is broken into three parts: Part I, which you are reading now, is the set up, giving you the background needed to start solving your business challenge. Part II is your step-by-step guide to true innovation. Part III gives you a few other things to think about that will help you in your innovation efforts.

Along the way, you'll see some important words of advice I want you to reproduce and paste onto your innovation wall (if you don't have an innovation wall, your bathroom mirror or the wall near your bed are perfect places to hang these innovation tidbits). You will find these innovation pearls in shaded "Helpful Hints" boxes like the one below.

HOW DO YOU LOOK AT THE WORLD?

Pretend you work in the accounting department at your company, and you see that the process of tracking the accounts receivables is very cumbersome. Your company uses Excel spreadsheets, and the same information is entered multiple times. When you mention it to your boss, he or she  retorts with: "Well, that's the way it was set up before I got here and it's working, so why change anything!"

Part of innovation requires you to look deep inside yourself. So let me ask you some very deep questions: "Are you the boss in this scenario?" "Is that something you might say?" The potential for innovation is all around you, but YOU are the one whose perspective has to be: "There has got to be a better way!"

I can't change your perspective; only you can! What I will give you are the tools and tips to come up with some great ideas — if you have the right perspective.

helpful hints

Chapter 2: Know What You Can Control (and What You Can't)

YOU CAN'T CONTROL YOUR BOSS (OR YOUR BOSS'S BOSS)

Even though I have been an executive at good-sized companies for many of the past 20-plus years, I have always made it a point to spend the time to learn and to understand the duties (and heavy lifting) required of the employees who report to me on a daily basis.

As a result, I realize that it would be naïve for me to think that if you come up with a great idea, you can then simply move forward and put it into action. In fact, you may be thinking: "Oh my gosh, I have a lot of great ideas, but my boss is an #?!&%#! and won't even listen to me!" Or maybe, your company has a stodgy, old-school mentality and is really set in the ways in which it does things. Well, I would like to tell you to find a better company to work for, but that's risky and not the point of this book (it would be nice, though, wouldn't it?).

Instead, I will tell you not to give up hope. The best thing you can do is take baby steps. Find small, incremental innovations that you can put into place. Ideally, find a small improvement that you can make all by yourself that has very little risk; do it, then bring it to your boss and say: "Hey, I just wanted you to know I changed the way we do this, and now it takes an hour less per week and is less likely to have any errors." Since it's already done, and it is working well and you have quantified an actual benefit, it would be very hard for your boss to say anything but: "Good job."

In this "worst case" type of environment, it's difficult to innovate because you don't control the culture of the company and you don't control your boss's personality. However, you *can* influence your boss, the people around you, and the company by taking these baby steps. Remember, even a small, incremental improvement is innovation!

And guess what: When the time comes for that promotion, you will be the more likely candidate to be promoted since you show initiative and the ability to manage change. Or, if you leave the company, you will have some good achievements to put on your resumé.

If you have to go with the "under the radar" approach because your company doesn't support innovation, I will give you some specific insights that I will highlight with this symbol:

YOU CAN'T CONTROL YOUR COMPANY'S CULTURE

I wanted to get into "culture" because it can be confusing for an employee (and even for the top executives in a company) to understand what culture is. So, let me try to explain the different kinds of cultures that may exist in a company. There are four types of culture: corporate, organizational, brand, and innovation. According to Wikipedia, the definitions for the first three types are as follows (I've edited them a bit):

Corporate culture is the total sum of the values, customs, traditions, and meanings that make a company unique. Corporate culture is often called "the character of an organization," since it embodies the vision of the company's founders. The values of a corporate culture influence the ethical standards within a corporation, as well as managerial behavior.

Organizational culture describes the psychology, attitudes, experiences, beliefs, and values (personal and cultural values) of an organization. It has been defined as "the specific collection of values and norms that are shared by people and groups in an organization and that control the way they interact with each other and with stakeholders outside the organization." Organizational culture is not the same as corporate culture. It has wider and deeper concepts; it is something that an organization "is" rather than what it "has."

Brand culture is a company culture in which employees "live" to brand values, to solve problems and make decisions internally, and to deliver a branded customer experience externally. It is the desired outcome of an internal branding or employee engagement effort that elevates beyond communications and training. A brand, in order to be relevant to consumers and sustainable over time, must operate much like a culture. A company must develop a worldview that it absolutely believes in and it should then act in accordance with it. Everything the company does — every product or service it offers, every public statement, advertisement, website, internal policy, memo, and business decision it makes — must be congruent with that worldview.

Innovation culture, defined by me, is the beliefs, values, and actions that a company takes to encourage the development and implementation of new ideas. This includes committing resources to innovation, adding innovation to its educational activities, having a tolerance for risk, accepting and even celebrating failure, and creating a structure to support the development of new ideas.

You can't control any of the above cultural aspects of your company, but once again, you can influence them. Specifically as it relates to innovation culture, you can educate yourself about innovation, instead of relying on your company to do it (in fact, that's exactly what you are doing now!). You can influence others by recommending they read this book (thanks!). You can follow the innovation processes in this book and take the baby steps mentioned at the beginning of this chapter. In turn, your actions and the positive results you generate will influence others. Maybe it will lead to that promotion, and then you will have more leeway to be even more innovative. You can communicate and market these achievements and build excitement about taking control over your own innovations.

YOU CAN'T CONTROL THE CREATIVITY OF PEOPLE AROUND YOU

There are many theories and concepts related to creativity, but one theory that I have personally found to be helpful was developed by Dr. Michael Kirton[1] in 1976. Dr. Kirton's Adaption-Innovation Theory is founded on the assumption that all people solve problems and are creative. However, the manner in which each person solves problems varies. According to Dr. Kirton's theory, a person will have a preferred approach to problem-solving, and he calls these people either adaptors or innovators.

Adaptors. Adaptors are described as those who would prefer to "do things better." They are most comfortable working within the existing framework, and they like structure. Dr. Kirton originally defined adaptors with the following descriptors: a) concerned with solving problems rather than finding them, b) seeking solutions to problems in tried and understood ways, c) maintaining high accuracy in long spells of detailed work, d) rarely challenging rules, e) sensitive to maintaining group cohesion, and f) providing a safe base for the innovator's riskier operations.

Innovators. Innovators are described as those who would prefer to "do things differently." They don't care about the existing framework or having structure around them. Dr. Kirton described innovators as: a) seemingly undisciplined; approaching tasks from unsuspected angles, b) treating accepted means with littler regard in pursuit of goals, c) capable of detailed tasks only in short bursts, d) providing the dynamics to bring about periodic revolutionary change, and e) having low self-doubt when generating ideas.

If you imagine a scale, with an extreme adaptor personality on one end and an extreme innovator personality on the other, you can envision that most people are not extremes but fall within a normal bell curve on the line between the two extremes. However, most folks will tend to gravitate toward one side or the other of the middle.

OK, why did I share all this with you? It's really important because if you start to think about the personalities of the people you work with, you can probably put them into one of these two camps. This is great on a day-to-day basis because you can go to the innovators when you need help coming up with some ideas in order to solve a business challenge, and you can tap into the adaptors when you have a need for detailed analysis and support.

Having an understanding of your co-workers' creative type also helps when you get around to putting together a project team for your innovation because you want to have both types on your team. You want the innovator who will help come up with additional modifications and adjustments to your idea that you are implementing. And, you definitely need the adaptor who will figure out and work on the 200 details that need to be taken into account to ensure your idea is successfully implemented.

You can read more about Dr. Kirton's theory at his official website at http://www.kaicentre.com. Go to the "About KAI" tab on the website to get more information. There's also a great PowerPoint presentation on this same website under the "KAI Materials" tab.

Chapter 3: Look Out for Land Mines!

I stand by the statement I made earlier: You can innovate no matter what your position is in your company. However, you will likely run into one or more land mines that may make innovating more difficult. You can navigate your way through the minefield without getting blown up, as long as you know where the mines are and you are very, very careful. Let's get into some of the details.

MONEY

Issue –

Money is definitely one of the top three potential land mines. Most companies keep a pretty tight rein on the wallet, and most of the time, some money will be needed to implement your great idea. Two things will stand in your way. First, in larger companies that  create a budget every year, there may not be any money budgeted to do what you want. That's a tough one. Second, money you want to spend on your idea may be competing against other potential projects that may already exist within the company.

Solution –

One way or another, you're going to be competing for dollars. So the best solution is to do your homework prior to presenting your project to your boss and/or upper management for approval. This means doing whatever research is necessary to support your project, and completing the project charter (see Chapter 7). The project charter includes an estimated return on investment (ROI), which is really important, since it's a common way for those finance types to compare one project against another.

Competing against other projects is similar to the often-told story about the two guys camping in the woods who see a bear approaching. The first guy immediately starts putting on his running shoes, yada, yada, yada, and he says: "I just have to run faster than you." Your ROI just has to be better than the other guy's to have a chance at getting money to fund your innovation.

PEOPLE

Issue –

You may need people to be part of your project team. You need a project leader (it could be yourself), you need someone with project management skills, and you need a project sponsor (someone with executive power to make sure you have the money, time, and other resources to make your idea reality). You also have to deal with people who operate in silos (those who don't help outside of their department) or who are self-centered (if it wasn't their idea, it's not a good one).

Solution –

If you have a small, incremental innovation that doesn't take a lot of work to put into action, you probably don't need a lot of people to help you. However, don't skimp on making sure you get a project sponsor. Usually in a company of any size, you will find kind people who are willing to help no matter how busy they are. You also will find people who get excited by new stuff and who want to be in on the action. In Chapter 7, I'll show you how to pick the right team and how to get these people on board. I'll also show you how to deal with the silos and the self-centered types.

TIME

Issue –

I am going to go out on a limb and assume that your job is keeping you plenty busy. OK, maybe you do a little surfing on the Internet, but only when you need to take a quick mental break from your work. Finding time to pursue innovation is difficult, especially in a company that is not supportive of new ideas.

Solution –

Look at all your regular duties; list them on a paper, if necessary. Then put them into the following categories:

- ☞ I have to do this task.
- ☞ I must do this task, but maybe I can find a way to do it faster.
- ☞ I can delegate this duty to someone else.
- ☞ I really don't have to do this task.
- ☺ If anyone gives me one more thing to do, I'm going to scream!

You can see where I'm going. I can almost guarantee that if you spend the time to really spell out in detail what you do, you'll find some things you don't need to do, or some you can delegate or make more efficient.

NO TOLERANCE FOR FAILURE

Issue –

A key part of an innovative culture is to accept failure as part of the risk-taking process that accompanies innovation. (See the Helpful Hint below for more discussion about this.) You may work for a company that frowns upon failure.

Solution –

I don't want you to get fired over a failed project. The key to avoiding this is to:

- ➤ Make sure you communicate the risks at the outset of the project (before it's approved).
- ➤ Communicate the status of your innovation effort on a regular basis as you work to turn your idea into reality.
- ➤ Follow the process outlined in this book to minimize the chance of failure.

> Be flexible and nimble enough to adjust what you are doing as you move your idea from concept to reality.

☺ Construct a secret compartment under your desk that you can hide in (do you remember this Seinfeld episode?).

SHORT-TERM PERSPECTIVE

Issue –

Even though you may not be an executive of your company or on the board of directors, it's good to know some of the pressures they may face. If you feel that your company is really pushing for immediate results, there could be a few reasons. If your company has publicly traded stock, it could be pressured to meet the outside analysts' quarterly forecasts. If a private equity firm owns your company, then your company's owner could be pressured to increase the company's value in time to sell it. You also may have a president who is just extremely action-oriented.

Solution –

If you feel you are under a lot of short-term pressures (if not sure, ask around), then it's important to take this into account during the part of the innovation process when you are filtering the ideas you came up with down to the best one. How quickly you can put this idea into action is one of the factors you will need to place a high priority on when you are in an environment where it's all about short-term results. We will talk more about filtering in Chapter 6.

COMPETING PROJECTS

Issue –

Many companies have a lot of projects (usually too many) hanging around. A common reason for this is that there is no approval or screening process for projects. Sometimes there is no one making sure a project fits within the strategic plan for the company (and/or the company doesn't even have a strategic plan). Or, it may be that projects don't have any structure around them, so there are no deadlines or measurements that determine success.

Solution –

The solution to this is similar to the one mentioned in the money section discussed earlier in this chapter. Your idea just has to be sexier than the other projects that are hanging around. If your innovation looks like it may be more profitable, has a better ROI, and has a higher likelihood of success, *and* if you show that you've done your research and have your act together, you are more likely to get approval and knock off one of the "Starving Monkey"[2] projects that are hanging around. Starving Monkey is a term created by William Oncken Jr. and Donald Wass that they wrote about in a time-management article published in the *Harvard Business Review* in 1974). For a really good description of the five Starving Monkey rules, refer to the *Information Week* article discussing it at the link listed in the Website References section at the end of this first book.

FAILURE IS AN OPTION[3]

> Don't fear failure! It's part of innovation! However, if you fail, make sure it's because you took a calculated risk, not because you didn't follow the process in this guide.
> It's human nature to tend to avoid challenges, not seek them out!
> Face the brutal facts, and do an autopsy without blame.

helpful hints

TOP REASONS FOR FAILED INNOVATION EFFORTS[4]

1. Wrong growth target (e.g., wrong customer, excluding an important customer)
2. Unfocused idea generation
3. Not enough or bad data
4. Ill-conceived growth strategy
5. Don't understand who your customer is (or could be)
6. Mistakes in prioritizing opportunities (i.e., making an improvement in an area that doesn't need it; making an improvement in an unimportant area; making an improvement that negatively affects other things that the customer values)

helpful hints

Part I   Action Summary

CHAPTER 1

- Go take a break and smell the flowers.

CHAPTER 2

- Write a list of things you can't control.
- Write a list of things you can control.

CHAPTER 3

- For each of the six "land mine" sections, write down any potential issues you may have at your company.

PART II – START INNOVATING

Now that you are set up for success, let's move on to the meat and potatoes of *Bottom-Up Innovation*: the four steps of innovation: Identify, Ideate, Filter, and Finish. Most people have a sense of the business challenge or problem they want to solve, so they will go right into the "Gathering Ideas" (I call it Ideate) phase. Oops! Big mistake!

In Chapter 4, we're going to spend some time identifying whether you are trying to solve the right challenge or issue. Then, in Chapter 5, we will move on to the fun part: coming up with ideas.

In Chapter 6, we'll take all those ideas you came up with and filter them down to the best one. This is another area where people tend to take a shortcut. It's too easy to select an idea to implement that you just happen to really like. Many small business owners prefer to use the "fly by the seat of the pants" method of selection. Oops! Another big mistake! It's a shame when people take the shortcut, because they are much more likely to end up with a result that is not as exciting as it could have been.

In Chapter 7, I'll go over a few things you need to know before you dive into the hard part of turning your idea into reality. Then, in Chapter 8, I'll walk you through project management lite — the process of making your innovation come to life ("Finish" phase)! Finally, in Chapter 9, I'll walk you through some things that can help you make sure your project finishes up beautifully and that your innovation is a success for you and your company.

Chapter 4: Identifying Your Business Challenge

So, what is your business challenge? The most typical issues that companies face are the following:

- ➢ Increasing sales
- ➢ Coming up with a new product or service
- ➢ Reducing expenses
- ➢ Improving profits
- ➢ Improving a process within the company
- ➢ Addressing a competitive threat
- ➢ Solving some other problem or issue that exists within the company
- ☺ Figuring out how to stop getting the air conditioning vent from blowing gale force winds right down on your cubicle

The second-to-last bulletpoint is purposely very broad, and it can deal with issues as diverse as employee morale and retention, accounts receivable collection issues, customer satisfaction, marketing ineffectiveness, or branding issues.

There is no challenge, problem, or issue that is too small to benefit from innovation. Remember, even if you are limited to what you can do based on what we discussed in Chapter 3, you can still innovate somewhere.

IDENTIFY YOUR CHALLENGE RULES

Remember these rules as you write down your challenge or problem:

- ➢ Try to address only the biggest issue (if you have multiple challenges, start with the one that is the weakest link). It's difficult to try to solve multiple things at once.
- ➢ Make sure your challenge is specific and clearly defined (e.g., "I'm not happy with my business" doesn't work).
- ➢ Make sure you quantify the challenge if at all possible (e.g., "I would like to increase sales of product X by 30 percent within 18 months").
- ➢ Think about whether solving this challenge achieves your goals.

➤ Make sure you have identified the cause of the challenge, not just a symptom (see examples of this below).

☺ Find someone in the company you don't like, and make sure you can place the blame on them if your innovation efforts fail.

WRITE DOWN YOUR CHALLENGE

Whatever your challenge is, write it down (if you are reading this on an e-reader or tablet, you can't easily print this page out, so just write your challenge down on a piece of paper). If you are reading this in a hard copy book, I suggest using a pencil, since you may want to modify this as we move forward.

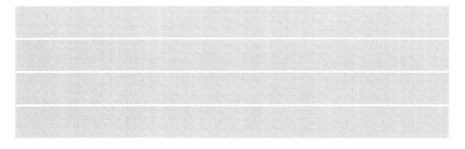

DON'T RUSH!

Are you sure you are trying to solve the right challenge? Let's say you had a pain on the side of your right hip. What were the symptoms? Let me guess, it hurt! Pain and soreness were the symptoms. So you took ibuprofen or went to the doctor to get muscle relaxers to ease the symptoms. It made you all better, right? Well, what *caused* this injury? Maybe you've been running a lot on roads that have an angle to them and that put a lot of stress on your hip. To eliminate the cause of the injury, you need to stop running on those angled roads. Many people, when trying to solve a business challenge, only see the symptoms of the issue. They don't spend the time to look beyond the symptoms to find a real cause.

Let me give you a few business examples that may help you open up your mind:

- ➤ Your sales are down (symptom). You think it's the economy, so you are thinking of a new type of marketing. But the real challenge is your company is bad at customer service (cause), and your customers are saying negative things about your company instead of recommending it to others.
- ➤ Your sales are down (symptom). You think it's the economy, so you are thinking of a new type of marketing. But the real challenge is that your competitors have improved their product or service (cause) and have left you behind.
- ➤ Your accounting staff's morale is down (symptom). You think it might be that the new controller is not providing the right kind of leadership. But the real reason is that your business is growing and they are feeling the pressure because they have a lot more transactions to process (cause).

After thinking about it, are you sure you wrote down the right challenge?

If not, and you feel that you know what the better challenge is, go back and fix it. If you are absolutely sure you've identified the business challenge you want to solve, jump ahead to Chapter 5. If you have any doubts whatsoever that your business challenge may need further refinement, keep reading.

SOLVING THE RIGHT CHALLENGE

There are a number of things you can do to make sure you are solving the right business challenge. The rest of this chapter will give you some different methods you can use to help you  dig into your challenge statement and make sure it's really, really good! You can use one of these methods, more than one, or all of them! It's up to you.

TALK IT OUT!

One of the most effective ways to make sure you're going after the right challenge is to talk to people. Who should you talk to?

- ☞ Talk to your fellow employees — they can often give you a perspective you can't see because you may be too close to the issue. Your fellow employees are one of your best resources to help you make sure you've nailed the challenge.
- ☞ Talk to your customers — you must have two or three customers who you really like and respect and have a good relationship with. Confide in them, and see what they say. Remember, if you work in an internal department, your customers may be fellow employees, other divisions of your company, or even your boss.
- ☞ Talk to your friends and family (the family may be the hardest part). This makes sense if the challenge is something they can relate to.
- ☞ Talk to your suppliers and vendors. They have a different perspective of your company that could be very helpful. They also may have some insight into similar challenges faced by other companies they do business with.
- ☞ Talk to your outside consultants (attorneys, accountants, marketing firm, etc.).
- ☞ Talk to any mentors with whom you've worked or become friends. How about anybody who may be a subject matter expert on your challenge?
- ☺ If nobody at all will listen to you, go down to the park with some bread and feed the pigeons. When they gather around you, explain your business challenge, and see if they have any thoughts.

Make sure you write down your discussions. In Appendix A, I have examples of pages that you can use to fill in the results of your work. You can also go to the Helpful Resources tab at www.simplyinnovate.net to find pdf copies of these forms that you can download and either fill out on your computer (they are in a fillable pdf format) or print out and use. Be sure to write down the name of who you talked to and any significant takeaways.

DO SOME RESEARCH

In addition to listening to your friends, customers, and business contacts, there are more ways to refine your business challenge. Don't be shy about doing some of these:

- Look at what your data is telling you (pull together some facts on the challenge that you have identified).
- Google your challenge on the Internet.
- Look to see if your competitors have similar issues. Talk to people who may work for your competitors, talk to vendors or customers of your competitors, research your competitors on the Internet, or visit them (if possible).
- Find out what your customers are saying online. If you operate retail locations, sites like Yelp or Google reviews, or even the feedback/comment section of your own website, are great places to find potential answers to what your real challenge is.
- If your challenge is part of a process, then write down all the steps in the process to see if you can isolate where the challenge occurs (e.g., if there is an issue in order fulfillment, break down all the steps from taking the order to delivery).

- Reword the challenge by looking at it from different angles. Find everyone who is touched or could be touched by this challenge, and put yourself in their shoes.
- ☺ Put your challenge on a billboard with your home phone number (preferably placed near a very busy freeway).

JOBS TO BE DONE[5]

In his book, *The Innovator's Solution*, Harvard Business School Professor Clayton Christensen states that customers buy products and services to help get a job done. This is a completely different mindset from how we usually look at any potential new innovation. We usually look at it from the point of what a customer needs. At first, that may sound like the same thing as "jobs to be done," but it is different. For example, if you have a plumbing leak, the plumber's perspective is that the customer needs to have the leak fixed. But if you look at it from a "jobs to be done" perspective, the homeowner wants to have a plumbing system that delivers consistent, worry-free hot and cold water. So if the plumber thinks of what job the customer needs to get done, he or she might suggest new products that help the homeowner from encountering plumbing problems in the future (e.g., annual pipe check, low-cost insurance for future repairs, etc.). Clayton Christensen can give you a better example than my attempt above. Check out his YouTube video at the website listed in the Website References at the end of this first book.

If you use this concept, first do your research, then write down the job to be done, and move forward and use the next technique before you sit down to evaluate and possibly revise your business challenge.

OUTCOME EXPECTATIONS

If you like the "jobs to be done" concept (which I do), then part of it is figuring out what the customer expects related to that job. This concept is called outcome expectations. Anthony Ulwick of Strategyn has trademarked a similar term called "outcome-driven innovation." You can listen to him talk about it on his YouTube video at the website link listed in the Website References at the end of this first book.

Using this technique, list the outcomes that the customer expects related to the job they want done. Then, think about your business challenge to see if it addresses what you have learned.

ETHNOGRAPHY (OBSERVATION)

According to answers.com, ethnography is the descriptive study of a particular human society based primarily on fieldwork. The ethnographer (observer) lives among the people who are the subject of study for a long period of time and participates in everyday life while striving to maintain a degree of objective detachment. He or she usually cultivates close relationships with the people being observed, those who can provide specific information on aspects of cultural life. While detailed written notes are the most important part of fieldwork, ethnographers also may use tape recorders, cameras, or video recorders.

It sounds easy, doesn't it? But, it's actually pretty hard to look at things from a fresh perspective and without any preconceptions. Imagine wiping your mind clean of any prior thoughts and opinions before you start observing. If you can do that, you'll be in a better place to pick up some new observations.

When it comes to innovation, the concept of observation is an important tool that can help you during the different steps of your innovating effort. The first time is right now! If you feel you've identified the business challenge, a good way to double check it is to spend time observing the people who are impacted by whatever you plan to innovate and documenting what you observe.

Scott Cook, the founder of Quicken, created a Follow Me Home program using observation that resulted in many of the company's new products and/or product improvements. Read about this program in an article on Inc.com. The website link is listed in the Website References section at the end of this first book.

A great example of using observation to innovate comes from a friend of mine who, for a number of years, worked in a local bicycle shop repairing bikes. Over time, he noticed that many customers were frustrated by the average week to 10-day turnaround for repairs. A lot of these folks only had one bike and liked to ride regularly. He also noticed that customers complained that prices were high for the repairs. He ideated a new concept: Open a shop that doesn't sell bikes, yet focuses only on repairs with a quick turnaround and lower prices. He opened that shop, committing to same-day or next-day service with prices up to 30 percent lower than the "normal" bike shops. And, by opening the shop in a light industrial area that had lower rent, he had extra space in the repair area for customers to come in and fix their own bikes using the shop's tools. Check out OC Bicycle Service + Garage at the company's website which is listed in the Website References section at the end of this book.

Observation is powerful. If you use this technique, make sure to take good notes on what you see! Stay tuned for more discussion, tips, and places you can observe in Chapter 5.

NAILING THE CHALLENGE

Did you make any changes to your challenge? If so, go back and revise your challenge statement. Don't forget to check your revised challenge statement against the rules at the beginning of Chapter 4.

Who's Right? Albert Einstein or Tony Robbins?

Albert Einstein once said, "If I had an hour to save the world, I would spend 59 minutes defining the problem and one minute finding solutions." Conversely, the popular motivational guru Tony Robbins has said, "Spend 20% of your time and energy in identifying the challenge, then spend 80% of your time finding the solutions."

Wow, they can't both be right, can they? I have to side with Albert in that many people think they are solving a problem, but are only addressing a symptom, or may not have identified the biggest problem. Generally, most people in business don't spend enough time at this stage.

My interpretation of what Tony is trying to address is the "stage fright" that some people get when trying to solve a problem. At some point, you have to believe you've done enough work to identify your challenge, and you need to take action to find solutions.

Chapter 5: Let's Ideate!

All right — here we go! We've identified the challenge; now let's come up with some ideas.

I'm going to give you four ways to come up with ideas: gather, observe, borrow, and brainstorm. The following pages will tell you how to use these methods to come up with ideas.

Before you start to ideate, read and use the idea-generating hints below to help you succeed in the idea-gathering phase. This is a list you may want to refer back to frequently as you use some of the approaches in this chapter to come up with ideas.

- ✗ Write down everything!
- ✗ Open your mind to new ideas (use music to help you; try Pandora, my favorite is a Dean Everson channel).
- ✗ Combine two or more things together to create something new (it is one of the most common ways to come up with new ideas).
- ✗ Draw stuff, and use visual aids as you are trying to make an idea come to life. If you are a doodler, you'll be great at this one.
- ✗ Think about a small, incremental improvement, and then go to the opposite extreme and think of something wild and wacky — breakthrough different. A lot of times, something in the middle that is pretty cool will pop out.
- ✗ Ask yourself: What is your point of differentiation? What can you do to stand out from the crowd?
- ✗ Your great idea should be something that you can do well. If you don't have the expertise (or don't think you can get it), then your idea may be hard to execute.

- Go for simplicity in design; stay focused. It's true that simple is often better.
- Remember that value has two sides of the equation. It's not only improved quality; it also can be lower cost. Customers may see a new product that has fewer bells and whistles at a much lower cost as a better value.
- Jump ahead and away from the competition by creating a leap in value (either higher quality or lower cost, as we talked about in the previous bulletpoint).
- Focus on what the customer needs to get done, not on what you offer.
- Identify the five most important things that your customers value.
- The perfect sweet spot is creating something that achieves your expectations and goals, as well as your customer's.
- Use the Internet to look at top 10 (or 100) lists (e.g., to come up with a name for a book, look at the top 1,000 movies of all time). This weird idea can take your mind in new directions.
- Challenge your assumptions. Write down what is limiting or restricting your idea, and then ask how it can be overcome.
- Think in reverse (e.g., how can I make my process slower?). Sometimes this triggers thoughts that take you in new and exciting directions.
- Create loafing time (see Helpful Hint below).
- Change your environment (my favorite ideating place is at a cliff overlooking the ocean). That old saying, "I need a change of scenery," can really help stimulate new ideas.
- Have fun; keep (or find) your sense of humor (LOL).
- Don't judge or critique your idea yet (you will do this in Chapter 6)!
- Answer these questions when trying to create something new: Can you adapt? Combine? Rearrange? Reverse? Magnify? Modify? Make smaller? Put to another use?

☺ Create a rock garden in your backyard with a log stump as a chair in the middle of this garden. Then, stare at the rocks.

Ideas Need to Simmer to Be Able to Morph Into Something New

I probably didn't explain well how the idea-gathering phase works. What you are doing in this section is collecting a lot of data. As you gather, observe, and borrow, you are seeing things that may be the seed of something new, but the idea is not yet there. That's OK. You need time to let all this stuff soak in. You also need to take some of the most interesting seeds, brainstorm, and talk about them with people you know. This doesn't happen overnight. Sometimes it can take weeks or even months.

GATHERING IDEAS

Gathering ideas is a great place to start when you are looking for something new. The list below shows a number of ways to generate lots of ideas. Read through this list, select two or three methods to start, and then do them!

 Remember, you may not immediately "see" the actual innovation as you are going through this process (if you do, awesome!), but you may see something that makes you sit up and say, "That's interesting; I should write this down." The "Aha!" moment, when the things you gathered morphs into something new, may happen later as you go back through your list (remember to sleep on it).

- ☐ Type the name of your challenge and/or industry into Internet search engines (Google, Yahoo, Bing); try many possible variations and keywords in your challenge.
- ☐ Find out which trade associations apply to your challenge or industry, and go to their websites, subscribe to their newsletters, and attend a conference if you are able.
- ☐ Email selected employees in your company and ask for ideas relating to your challenge. Make sure in your email that you are specific enough about what the challenge is, and then ask them not to censure themselves; it doesn't matter how silly an idea may seem (the time for filtering and modifying will come later). Also, make sure you recognize anybody who contributes ideas by, at the very least, sending a nice thank-you email back (or, you can be more creative and send them a thank-you e-card).
- ☐ Email selected vendors, customers, friends, etc., using the same rules as the previous bulletpoint. Of course, before doing this, be sure the challenge is something that is OK to share outside of the company.

- Even better than email, meet with individuals and talk about what you are trying to solve.
- Post a challenge on Facebook if you have a group of friends and if the challenge is something that is OK to share outside of the company.
- Use crowdsourcing sites such as www.innocentive.com (Google the definition of crowdsourcing if this term is new to you). You can keep the challenge non-specific so they can't identify your company.
- Look for online webinars for your industry that might have topics that can plant the seed of an idea.
- Read trade magazines or books that relate to your industry or the challenge that you have.
- Look for industry analyses such as published reports and surveys on the Internet. Better yet, I can almost guarantee that somebody in your company has some industry reports that could be useful to you, and you just don't know it. Ask around; you'll be surprised what you find.
- Look for things that just are not done in your industry. One way is to pick a random industry, and find out (either through the Internet or other methods) how it handled a similar issue (it doesn't have to be the same issue; it could be the closest thing you can find to the issue you have). Then, look at what it has done to resolve it. You also can look at what that industry does very well. Any of these things may give you ideas.
- Come up with a list of five ways to change your product to make it more appealing. One way to do this is to list all the adjectives you can think of that may be associated with the process, product, or service that is part of your challenge (e.g., red, angular, heavy, responsive, friendly, expensive, etc.). Then, use opposites of these adjectives, and/or use different adjectives that are in the same family (e.g., attentive instead of friendly) to help you come up with some new ideas.
- Look at five to 10 innovations in your industry (both successful ones and not so successful ones); figure out common elements of the successful innovations vs. failed efforts. This may give you some good ideas for your challenge.
- ☺ Go on a world cruise for the next two years, spending time in as many countries as you can (OK, I really want to do this one).

Make sure you write down all the ideas you gather. In Appendix A, there are pages you can use to write down your ideas. You also can go to the Helpful Resources tab at www.simplyinnovate.net to find copies of these forms that you can use.

Where Do People Come Up with Their Best Ideas?

Do this! Ask your friend to name what physical place they are in when they come up with their best ideas. Ninety-five percent of them will name one of these four places: driving, in bed (sleeping or dozing), in the shower, working out.

So, anytime you are going to ask people to help you figure something out, whether it's helping you identify the challenge (Chapter 4) or during a brainstorming session, tell them a few days before you meet what the challenge is and that you will be looking for them to bring some ideas to the meeting. That way, they will be thinking about this while they are driving, working out, etc.

That makes a lot of sense, doesn't it? It's amazing how few people do this!

Likewise, as you are going through this step, don't try to do everything in one day. Spend some time sleeping on it; go mountain biking (my favorite) or walking, or take a drive. You need time for all the info you've gathered to absorb in your subconscious and percolate back up with new insights.

View the YouTube video by Dr. Sanjay Gupta that supports the above concept with some research. The link to this video can be found in the Website References section at the end of this first book.

helpful hints

BORROWING IDEAS

Borrowing ideas may sound like stealing. It's not; it's creative theft. No, it's not even that. Many of the best ideas come from taking something that exists and making it better. Borrowing does not mean outright copying something that exists today. It is about taking the idea and using it to create something that is clearly your own. This section has some elements that are similar to the gathering and observing phase, but the concept is different enough that it's worthy of discussion in its own right.

In *The Origin and Evolution of New Businesses*,[7] Amar Bhide says that "more than two-thirds of his entrepreneurs replicated or modified ideas encountered through previous employment." David Kord Murray's more recent book, *Borrowing Brilliance*,[8] does a great job of capitalizing on this concept. In this book, Murray suggests that innovations result from borrowing ideas from different disciplines, putting them together, and building on them. According to Murray: "Great ideas are built on the ideas of others."

Another great book, *Strategic Intuition*[9] by William Duggan, discusses the discipline of great idea formulation and how creativity and rational thinking combine in the mind to achieve this. My favorite example in this book is how Napoleon Bonaparte in the 1800s borrowed ideas to create something new. Napoleon was known for flashes of insight throughout his life. He had extensive knowledge of the great military achievements of the past, and he drew from these for his strategy formulation.

Napoleon's own winning military ideas combined elements well known at the time — none of which he invented — into a winning formula. They included studying contour maps of the region, the use of the light cannon that could be transported for battle anywhere, and knowledge of every great military conquest in history and how it was won. Due to his study of military history, Napoleon had many possible elements to draw from. This unique combination of information from the shelves of his mind, and not only from his own experience, formed his winning military strategy. You could say that Napoleon borrowed ideas of battle and strategy from many prior generals, as well as ideas on the use of weaponry, to come up with something new and very effective (until Waterloo, that is).

So, enough of the introduction. What are some of the ways you can fill out your idea list by borrowing?

- Think about your previous jobs. Is there something you can use and modify from that experience? This can be one of your best borrowing sources!
- Take something that you see a competitor doing that you really like, and break that product, service, or process into as many component pieces as possible. Then, use pieces of it (not the whole thing) to make something new.
- Go to two or more different competitors and find products, services, or processes that could address the challenge you have. Then, take the best of each of them (maybe adding something new to the mix) in order to make something new. Visualize making a pot of stew. The individual ingredients may be OK on their own, but mixed together with some spices added and a dash of loving care, you have a great-tasting meal.
- Look at your competitors. Check out their leaders and what they are doing right; then, look at the laggards and what they are doing badly. You can get inspiration from both.
- Make a list of all the remarkable products in your industry. Who made them? Why are they successful? How did that happen? Is it possible that something can come along to make them obsolete? What would that be?
- Look for industry blogs, and see if they are discussing anything that could be useful to take and modify.
- If you can't find ideas in your industry, go to other industries. Start with related industries, and find a company that stands out. Even unrelated industries may have ideas because they may have a process or service issue that is similar to what you are trying to solve. It doesn't even have to be very similar. Sometimes, things you see that are only in the general ballpark

of what you are looking for can give you a unique idea that could be the one!

🐙 Don't just sit in your office or home; get out and see what's going on!

🐙 Make sure you write down all the ideas that come out of your efforts above.

☺ Borrow sugar from your neighbor, money from your brother, a pen from your co-worker, and a cigarette from the tough-looking dude on the street corner.

The Two Sides of Customer Feedback

Your customers are a valuable resource, especially when you are defining your challenge. It's important to talk to them during the idea phase, but it's important to realize that although they have possible solutions to a challenge, they are not always experts in your business and may not have the best solution. Customers are also usually not great at verbalizing what they need. That's why it's more important to look at what the customer is trying to get done and what that customer values highly in a product or service. It is also why observing (see the next section) is such a valuable idea-generation tool.

helpfulhints

OBSERVING

Some of your best ideas can come from watching. It could be watching your employees, your customers, your competitors, your non-customers, your family, your dog, or your goldfish.

"Wow," you're thinking, "finally something I can do. I can look at things." But there are secrets below that will help you be a better watcher and give you ways to observe and come up with ideas. Read Chapter 4 on ethnography again if you are going to use observation to come up with ideas.

- Follow a customer home, to their work, or wherever they use your product or service (with their permission), and watch them in action. See what they do, what their needs are, and what you can do to help them in new ways.
- If the challenge you have is an internal challenge, use the previous bulletpoint to watch how other employees interact with the process or service that is relevant to your challenge.
- Uncover what comes naturally to people as it relates to a product, service, or process. Then, do some "what if" scenarios; change some of the rules or constraints that currently exist. What would happen then?
- Keep a truly open mind; it's not easy, but try to pretend you are looking at this product, service, or process for the first time. Note all the details, every little way it's used, no matter how trivial. Look at the reactions or comments of the people who interact with it.
- Write down a list of bugs or issues that you see when you are observing. This list can trigger some new ideas.
- Don't just watch customers; watch non-customers, too (can you offer them something to make them your customers?).
- Conduct thorough interviews and/or focus groups (this requires expert help and can cost a bit of money). Focus groups are helpful only to a degree; a good moderator can get some good information, but because of the structure of the focus group, it can be biased due to the personalities in the room and the conference room setting.
- ☺ If you've tried all these observation methods and nothing is working and you are desperate, then you might as well give up and go to the www.peopleofwalmart.com website and observe some entertaining people.

You've got to get out of the office or house to observe! Go, get out now!

Make sure you write down all the ideas you gather.

How to Improve Your Vision

> ➢ When you observe something, ask specific questions. Get in the habit of asking "why?" Don't let up until you get to the core of the issue.
> ➢ Ask open-ended questions (not closed-ended that can be answered with a "yes" or "no"). Start with: "Tell me about...." Look for behaviors and things people are doing because they may be working around an issue or challenge that they have with your product.
> ➢ Remember, observing helps you identify needs and solve challenges that the customer may not recognize. You will need to recognize what those are, and then ask questions to get the details.
> ➢ You may still need to brainstorm, gather, or borrow if you observe something big but you're still not quite there with the actual idea.

helpfulhints

BRAINSTORMING

Brainstorming is simply getting a few people together and then using them to come up with ideas. Brainstorming can be conducted as your primary idea-generating method. Or, because you may have some interesting ideas but still need help fleshing them out into something truly innovative, brainstorming can be used after your idea-gathering, borrowing, or observing efforts. The brainstorming tips below are important, as they will help you in your brainstorming session.

Read the tips below. Then, further down on the next page, I'll show you how to hold informal and/or formal brainstorming sessions.

Brainstorming Tips

- ✗ IMPORTANT: Make sure you tell the people who will be involved with your brainstorming session what the business challenge is that you are trying to find an innovation for. Read the Helpful Hint "Where Do People Come Up with Their Best Ideas?" earlier in this chapter.
- ✗ Assemble a diverse group of people, including people outside your company. If you want a variety of ideas, you need a variety of people.
- ✗ Two to four is the optimal number of people for casual brainstorming; five to 10 people is the optimal number for formal brainstorming.
- ✗ Go for quantity; get lots of ideas. You don't want to limit input at the first phase of your brainstorming session.
- ✗ Try to keep the session to a maximum of 90 minutes.
- ✗ Post ideas all over the room or area you are using (for formal brainstorming only).
- ✗ Keep the energy up, and keep the attitude positive.
- ✗ Don't judge or criticize ideas; this can be difficult because it's natural for people to jump in and start evaluating. As the leader, it's your responsibility to keep things under control.
- ✗ It is OK in the meeting for people to build on ideas; you can promote this by saying: "I like it; anybody have any ideas on how can we make it even better?"
- ✗ Tell people at the start that as people throw out their ideas, it may trigger additional ideas (or variations of an idea) in their minds. Ask them to write those down, and tell everyone they'll get a second chance to throw in those ideas (don't forget to do this).

- ✗ Get everyone to speak; there's usually at least one meeting-takeover artist and one quiet-as-a-mouse type. As the leader, it's your responsibility to manage this (as nicely as possible).
- ✗ Have the group do homework: Visit a place, read something, bring something (pictures, anything).
- ✗ Stay focused and on target. You've got only 90 minutes. Don't let the conversation stray.
- ✗ Look for breakthrough improvements, as well as incremental improvements.
- ☺ If you get stuck at any point in your brainstorming session, try to reinvigorate the session by asking: "What would SpongeBob and Patrick do?"

After you have your initial boatload of brainstormed ideas, use the following tips:

- ✗ Eliminate bad ideas quickly (if in doubt, keep the idea alive for now because you will be officially filtering them down in the next step).
- ✗ Take the best ideas, and try to make them better.
- ✗ One way to make an idea better is to determine whether the idea is SMART (specific, measurable, achievable, realistic, time-bound).
- ✗ Make sure you write down all the ideas that survive your discussion (if in doubt, keep the idea alive at this point).

Casual Brainstorming

Casual brainstorming is simply getting together with a couple of people over coffee or lunch to talk about your challenge and come up with some ideas. You won't be posting notes all over the walls or using brainstorming methods, but most of the tips on the previous page should apply.

To have a casual brainstorming session:

1. Select the people, invite them to coffee or lunch, outline the business challenge for them, and let them know you'd like them to come to the meeting with some ideas.

2. At the meeting place, let them know the relevant ground rules discussed previously.
3. Ask for ideas that they have brought with them.
4. You should have a good list of ideas. Now, ask them if they have any other ideas that came to them as they were listening to other people present their brainstorms or variations on ideas that were presented.
5. As a group, try to build on the ideas, and discuss the ones that seem to have the most traction.
6. Try to get a sense of which ideas get the most enthusiasm.
7. Take tons of notes.

Formal Brainstorming

Formal brainstorming is held in a private location (like a conference room) where you can assemble a larger group of people, talk with freedom, and post notes all over the walls. You also may use some of the brainstorming methods that are discussed on the next page. Items you will need for the session include easel paper, markers, tape you can use on walls, and drinks.

To conduct a formal brainstorming session:

1. Select the people, invite them to the meeting, outline the business challenge for them at least two days before the meeting, and let them know you'd like them to come with some ideas.

2. At the meeting, introduce everyone to each other if some are strangers.
3. Let them know the ground rules (make sure you pre-write them from the tips above).
4. Outline the business challenge.
5. Ask for any ideas that were brought; write them on the easel paper, and post them on the walls.
6. Ask them if they have any other ideas or variations on ideas that were presented.
7. Use one or more of the brainstorming methods below, and then add any ideas that come up as a result (you probably have time for only one or two methods).
8. Ask the group to try to build on the ideas; add these to the notes on the walls.
9. Have everyone write down on paper their top-three ideas and turn them into you.

Tabulate results, share them with the group, and thank them for their help.

Brainstorming Methods

There are a lot of brainstorming methods, many of which can get quite complicated. Some of the easier ones that you can learn and use in your formal brainstorming session are Scamper, Hit Matrix, Random Word, SWOT analysis, and Brainwriting. I don't want to spend valuable book paper getting into the details of these when you can easily find them on the Internet or in other books that focus on brainstorming techniques. You also can go to my website, www.simplyinnovate.net, and look under the Helpful Resources tab for brainstorming references.

HOW TO KILL A BRAINSTORMING SESSION

⚡ Have the boss or leader (that's probably you) speak first with his or her ideas and make everyone feel intimidated.

⚡ Include only experts in the group; don't have a diverse group of people.

⚡ Make it serious; no laughing, smiling, or jokes allowed.

⚡ Have someone dominate the discussion (you know there's always someone who will if you let them).

⚡ Don't write everything down (use your infallible memory).

helpfulhints

Chapter 6: Filter Those Ideas!

It's really easy to select an innovative idea that you just happen to really like. Many small business owners prefer to use the "fly by the seat of the pants" method of selection. It's a shame, because they are much more likely to end up with a result that is not as exciting as it could have been. If at all possible, recruit a couple of your fellow employees to help you filter ideas. And, try to select people who seem to have a healthy dose of creativity. It always helps to have multiple minds talking about the ideas. You may even further improve some ideas during the filtering process!

BASIC FILTERING

The most popular filtering measurements are effort, profit, cost, and expertise. Here's a better explanation of these four measurements:

- Effort – How much heavy lifting will be required? How long will it take? Will it involve a lot of people to make it happen?
- Profit – How much money will you make (profit is revenue less ongoing expenses)? Does it have a high return on investment?
- Cost – Will this be expensive to implement? The ongoing costs shouldn't be part of this measurement, as they have been taken into account in your profit calculation above.
- Expertise – Do you already have the expertise to implement this new innovation? If not, will you need to bring in outside expertise, or will you need to have training or education to get up to speed?

Filtering is relatively easy. Just rate your ideas on a form like the example below from one to three. The higher the total, the better the idea looks.

Here is the scale to use:

Effort:	1=Hard	2=Medium	3=Easy
Profit:	1=Low	2=Medium	3=High
Cost:	1=High	2=Medium	3=Low
Outside Help:	1=Lots	2=Some	3=None

You may need to analyze and research some of your ideas further before you start the filtering process. This is really important because you want your ranking to be as objective as possible.

See an example of the filtering form in Appendix A. You also can go to the Helpful Resources tab at www.simplyinnovate.net to find a copy of this form that you can fill in on your computer or print out and use.

ADVANCED FILTERING

You might decide that some of the factors on the previous form deserve to be weighted more heavily than others. If so, you can change the points given to that factor. You also may decide that a factor isn't important to you. If not, don't use it.

If you decide to add some other factors, some popular ones include:

- Is this idea unique?
- Does it give the company a leg up on its competitors?
- Will it create efficiencies?
- Do you have the technical competency?
- Do you have the business competency?
- Is it a strategic fit with the company?
- How risky is it?
- Does it have competitive sustainability?

🦴 Will it be a challenge to market?
☺ Does it go well with a nonfat café mocha?

If you want to do some advanced filtering, go to the Helpful Resources tab at www.simplyinnovate.net, and find the advanced filtering form. If you have more than four factors you want to weigh, use additional forms for the additional factors, then total the pages together to get an overall ranking.

Chapter 7: Pre-Implementation Checklist

Pre-congratulations! You've got a cool idea that you believe can be an innovation that has value for your company. You've done a lot of work to get to this point, but there is still some heavy lifting to do. In this chapter, we're going to talk about some of the things you need to think about when starting a project, which is what you are doing now. Don't worry. I'll walk you through it the rest of the way. Before you begin trying to implement this idea, let's go over few important things you need to think about before you start this phase. You also might want to go back and skim the land mines in Chapter 3 as some of them become more relevant here.

EXECUTIVE SPONSOR

This is the time (if you haven't done it earlier) to line up your executive sponsor. Who is this person? It should be someone in the organization pretty high up in the pecking order. The higher his or her position, the better. He or she needs to be someone who is part of the executive team or, at the very least, someone who has regular communication with an executive team member. This person has to be someone who is a straight shooter and who is not going to throw you under the bus if things don't go well (remember, failure is a part of innovation).

A project without executive sponsorship (support) is like skydiving without a parachute! You have the same chance of success (Travis Pastrana is crazy (and a stud)).

What does this person do for you and your innovation efforts? These are the key things you want your executive sponsor to do:

➢ Provide guidance on how to best position the project for approval.
➢ Help you understand any corporate dynamics that might undermine your innovation efforts.
➢ Sponsor your project through the approval process (discussed later in this chapter).
➢ Free up the big three things needed to gain innovation success: money, time, and people (either internal employees or external consultants).
➢ Help clear any roadblocks that may surface as you go through the process.
☺ Help get you an audition for the new reality show, "Undercover Innovator."

Your responsibility is to make sure you utilize your executive sponsor without driving him or her crazy. The best way to do this is to make sure you do everything you can (from a research and effort standpoint) to have your work done before you ask for help. For example, make sure you complete the project charter, and put together your thoughts on how much of the big three resources you will need. Also, try to schedule meetings wisely, saving non-critical issues for later, if possible (it may not always be possible if something critical pops up).

Under the Radar Tip: When don't you need an executive sponsor? Well, we talked about how if you happen to work for a company that is the polar opposite of innovative, your best bet is to find those small incremental innovations that can improve a process, add some efficiency, or save a little money. If you've found something like this to innovate, and you are sure it's a very low-risk initiative and doesn't need any money or outside resources, you can just go forward and do it (it's always good to get your boss's approval). Don't skimp on any of the other steps, but you're probably fine without the executive sponsor.

PLANNING

Here's a quick pop quiz to determine your personality type: When you read the word planning, did you cringe? If so, you likely found it easier and more fun to come up with ideas that probably fall into the "outside the box" innovator group we talked about in Chapter 2. That means digging into the details is not your specialty. If this is true, you need to either fight against your inner urges and spend some time in this section, or find someone to help you.

Planning is incredibly important; it is what will make sure you can take your idea and turn it into a profitable success. We will start planning in this section by completing a relatively simple, but powerful form called the project charter. I also like to call this the "idea to action summary sheet," as it is a crucial link in taking your idea and moving it along the path to reality.

PROJECT CHARTER

Many people will skip the project charter. Big mistake! This is your compass; you will always be able to go back to this to make sure you're heading in the right direction.

The version of the project charter I have below is one I have used at a number of companies I have worked for. The strength behind this version is its simplicity, which means it is more likely to be used. Its weakness is that it doesn't cover some things that might be helpful in more complex projects. To obtain a fill-in version of this form, go to the Helpful Resources tab at www.simplyinnovate.net. If you have a more complex project, you can Google "project charter" on the Internet to see if there are any other versions out there that may be better for yours.

Sample Project Charter

Project Purpose/Goal

Why are you doing this? To...

Key Objectives

What two to four things do you plan to do? They are...

Measures of Success

You know you have succeeded when...

Project Team

Who is going to do it?

Risk Assessment

What are the biggest risks with this project?

Project Budget (estimated)

Up-front costs:

Ongoing costs:

Profit estimate, year 1:

Profit estimate, year 2 (without up-front costs):

Return on investment:

PROJECT APPROVAL

All right, let's get this baby approved so you can implement your innovation. If your company has its act together, it may have a well-known process that you need to follow in order for your project to be approved. If not, then you are going to have to put something together. The more sophisticated and the better researched, the more likely you are to get that approval you are looking for. What do you need? Here's the list:

1. Start with a summary of your innovation. Include what the idea is, what the benefit is to the company, what research you did, why this idea should see the light of day, and why it is more important than other projects.

2. Include the project charter you completed in the previous step.

3. Include the support behind how you calculated the budget information in the project charter. Unless you just guessed at the numbers, you probably put together an Excel spreadsheet. List any assumptions that you made in coming up with the numbers. If you are not a finance person, get some help if you need it.

4. What's worse, going overbudget or presenting a lower return on investment because you were low on estimated costs? The easy

answer is: Don't go overbudget. Err on the side of estimating higher on the costs. It's better to be conservative than to lose your job because you were too aggressive.

5. If needed, go into more detail in the risk assessment. Talk not only about the risks, but what you believe may minimize these risks.

6. Optional: If you are good at PowerPoint presentations and you will be asked to present this project to a group, most of the above (with supporting handouts as necessary) can fit well into a presentation.

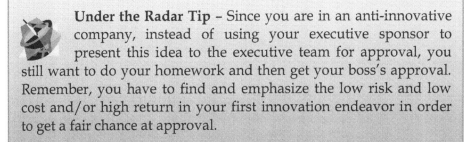

Under the Radar Tip – Since you are in an anti-innovative company, instead of using your executive sponsor to present this idea to the executive team for approval, you still want to do your homework and then get your boss's approval. Remember, you have to find and emphasize the low risk and low cost and/or high return in your first innovation endeavor in order to get a fair chance at approval.

PROJECT TEAM

Who do you need on your project team? Well, that depends on the size and scope of the idea you want to implement.

If it's a small incremental improvement that is quick and easy to implement, you may be able to do it all yourself. If so, you can move on to the next section.

However, if it's a bigger project, then you need some more help. Let's start at the top. First, you need a project leader. What does a project leader do?

I'm glad you asked. The project leader:

- Picks the project team.
- Leads the team.
- Has ultimate responsibility for the project.
- Executes the project plan.
- Is the morale maintainer, motivator, and roadblock identifier.
- Makes sure communication happens within the project team and with the executive sponsor.
- ☺ Stresses over the project by pacing the hallways, wringing their hands, drinking excessive caffeine, eating too many cupcakes, and having extreme insomnia.

There's more to this list below, but I want to stop here to let you know that many times, either as project leader or executive sponsor of a project, I have found that the best thing we ever did was to add a project manager to work with the project leader. What's the difference? Well, here's the rest of the list that is ultimately the responsibility of the project leader, but could be performed by a project manager. The project manager:

- Creates a detailed project plan, including all the major and minor steps.
- Creates a timeline to accomplish all the steps.
- Schedules all the meetings.
- Holds the team accountable to the timetable by getting time commitments and immediately identifying any lapsed deadlines.
- Puts checkpoints in place to measure the project against budget and other success criteria.
- ☺ Uses sophisticated project management tools and terminology that no one else on the team can understand and use.

We found that many very smart and talented people never really develop the skills necessary to handle the second part of the list above. Sometimes, even when the project leader has the skills to do everything, they don't have the time to do everything. Therefore, for larger projects, we actually went outside and hired a project manager because we did not have anybody in-house who had the expertise to complete all the tasks

For the rest of the project team, having people with the required expertise (and time) to support the project is very important to its success. Many times this means finding people from different departments and even outside consultants. Also, a good mix of creative types and detailed experts (remember Chapter 2) is essential. As an example, a project I sponsored at a restaurant included individuals from the IT, HR, operations support, accounting, franchise, and training departments, as well as a district manager and two general managers.

Chapter 8: Implementing Your Ideas

Great! You've done the planning. Your project has been approved. You've got the team assembled. What do you do now? Before I give you the step-by-step instructions to complete this project, it's important to know how you will outline the details for what needs to be done.

Top 10 Reasons Projects Fail

Careful planning and attention will help prevent the following 10 causes of project failure, according to Danek Bienkowski in his article Ten Causes of Project Busts:[10]

- The project is a solution in search of a problem.
- Only the project team is interested in the end result.
- No one is in charge (or the person in charge is not effective).
- The project plan lacks structure.
- The project plan lacks detail.
- The project is underbudgeted.
- Insufficient resources are allocated.
- The project is not tracked against its plan.
- The project team is not communicating.
- The project strays from its original goals.

PROJECT PLAN DETAIL

To carry your idea to the finish line, you need a detailed project plan. If you or someone on your team knows Microsoft Project, awesome! This software is specifically designed to track all the steps of a project, including due dates and priorities. If you don't have a Microsoft Project expert, I would suggest you at least use Excel. Go to the Helpful Resources tab at www.simplyinnovate.net for a blank spreadsheet you can use and for an example of how it looks filled out.

MAJOR STEPS

List the major steps associated with your project. Once you write them down, number them in the order you will complete them (some things can't be done before others). Don't worry if you have to come back and revise this.

MINOR STEPS

Start by writing down the No. 1 major step from the previous page; then, underneath it, list all the minor steps that need to be completed in order for the major step to be completed. These minor steps are the actions you will take to put your innovation in place. For each minor step, you will list a start date and an end date, who is responsible, and any precedent steps that need to occur prior to that step. Write down the minor steps for each of the major steps. You may need a number of pages for this.

GET THE PROJECT GOING!

Let's get that team working for you. Here's your schedule to turn this idea into success:

- Schedule your first team meeting. The purpose of this meeting is to go over the project in detail (use the information you created to get the project approved; this is where the PowerPoint comes in handy if you created one).

- Make sure that in this meeting you lay down the ground rules. Some rules you might want to consider are:
  - Members will be at all meetings (except for illness and emergencies). If you can't attend, notify the facilitator in advance.
  - Agendas will be distributed at least one day before each meeting.
  - Meetings will start and end on time.
  - The group will listen respectfully to the opinions of all team members by:
    - Using active listening.
    - Not using "killer phrases" or negative body language.
    - Brainstorming without editing.
- Emphasize to the team members the importance of meeting minor step deadlines. If a deadline needs to be moved, the project manager should be informed as early as possible. Look at the brainstorming meeting tips in Chapter 5 for some other tips that may help.
- By this meeting, you should have outlined the major steps (you may not have them all, buy that's OK). You will ask the team members to fill in all the remaining steps over the next week. Some of these may be discussed in the meeting; take note of them.
- Once you have the major steps and minor steps documented, email this Microsoft Project sheet (convert it into a pdf file if not all team members have the Microsoft Project software) or Excel spreadsheet to all the team members, and ask them to begin working on their steps.
- Encourage informal meetings/hallway discussions between the regularly scheduled meetings when two or more team members need to work out an issue.
- Hold weekly meetings (or every two weeks), but lay down these ground rules:
  - Any updates to the minor steps (completion, deadline changes) have to be communicated to the project manager before the meeting.
  - Any issues (action items) that a team member needs the group's input on should be communicated to the project

manager before the meeting and included on the agenda for that meeting.

    o   The meeting length should be no more than one hour.

    o   The purpose of the meeting is to discuss and resolve any issues/action items. It is *not* intended for everyone to go around the room and say what they are doing.

➢ Make sure you communicate with your executive sponsor regularly. But, communicate immediately when you see a change in the budget, risk assessment (chance of failure), or timeline change, or if you need their roadblock-clearing help.

Keep your attention on the details above, make sure you hold your team accountable, and maintain a positive atmosphere. After all, you are innovating, and it should be fun!

Under the Radar Tip – Just a reminder: If it's an incremental innovation that doesn't need a lot of interdepartment support, you may not need to put together a formal team. This is more the exception than the rule, so make sure you don't set yourself up to fail by not putting a team together.

CHECKPOINTS

It's good practice to build some checkpoints into your process. There should be at least three or four times during the process when you, with your team, decide if "all systems are a go." It's similar to what pilots do before they land: They check all the systems to make sure they are going to have a smooth and successful landing. These checkpoints usually occur after the completion of some major step, after testing, prior to full rollout, or after a significant hurdle is faced.

Learn More about Project Management

- To learn more about project management, there's a great slideshow at http://www.score.org/resources/guide-project-management.
- You can also check out this website: http://management.about.com/od/projectmanagement/ht/ProjMgt Steps.htm
- There also are two books I like best. My favorite, which has been around since 1992, is *5-Phase Project Management* by Joseph W. Weiss and Robert K. Wysocki.[11] This book is relatively concise (at about 100 pages) and very helpful. The *Project Management for Dummies* book by Stanley E. Portny[12] also is good.

Chapter 9: Rollout and Beyond

Your idea is now turning into reality. You have completed or you are close to completing all the steps necessary to bring this idea to life! Where do you go from here?

TEST

If possible, you want to test your idea before you fully implement it. While this may not always be possible, at least be prepared to adjust what you've done based on the results you see and the feedback you get.

If it's a product, create a prototype and have a couple of customers try it. If it's a service, outline the concept and try it out on a customer you know well. If it's a change to a process, test it by running the new process alongside the old process (this is called parallel testing). This way, if something bad happens with the new process, the old process is still working, and you haven't created havoc. If this is not possible, then you want to make sure you simulate the new process by walking through every step of it to see where something might go wrong.

Please take a minute and go to the "Value of Testing" section in Chapter 8 of *Top-Down Innovation*. This chapter has some additional advice about the importance of testing, as well as some resources you can use.

ROLLOUT

A big part of your success with something new is how well you implement it (think of wowing your customers) and how well you market it (I hope you addressed this in one or more of your steps).

There are a couple different ways to roll out something new. The first is a soft rollout, where you don't support the introduction of your new product, process, or service with any marketing, public relations, or internal communications. This is a good way to proceed when you feel that you have some kinks to work out and if you have new people involved with the rollout who need some time to get up to speed and become efficient. Basically, you will still complete the promotional items; you will merely defer them for a little while.

The other way to roll out something new is to do it with a bang. Plan your promotional activities to support the introduction of your innovation. You will likely have a surge of promotional activity when you first launch the concept, and then provide ongoing support as you move forward.

GET FEEDBACK (AND USE IT)

Go out of your way to get comments about your new innovation. If it is a customer-focused innovation, put a blog on your website, and follow up on emails, postcards, discounts for future products, etc. If customers fill out a  survey, summarize the feedback to see where you can improve.

If it's an internal innovation, get early and continued feedback from the employees and other people who are affected by this new innovation. Make sure you thank them for their feedback, no matter what it is.

ADJUST AND REFINE

 Don't rest yet; to keep profits flowing in, be ready to adjust what you have done to make it even better. It is pretty rare that a new innovation hits the success bulls-eye the first time. Often, once you see your innovation in action, the feedback you get, along with your and your project team's observations, will result in a list of adjustments and refinements. That's fine; use the process in this guide a second time if you need to.

MONITOR AND MEASURE

YOU DID IT! But wait, there's one more thing. It's good to go back and look at the project charter you created in Chapter 7 to see if your idea met the goals you set. If it did, great! If not, you might want to adjust your idea, or you might not have really succeeded (sorry, I don't want to bring you down, but failure is part of innovation).

You have created something new, and like a newborn baby, you can't leave it to its own devices, or it may crawl out in the middle of the street and get hit by a car. There are a lot of things that can derail what looks like a great start to a new product. This list could include product defects, lack of training, competitor actions, and even internal sabotage due to jealousy or power struggles. Stay on top of your new baby, and you'll be fine.

CLOSING ASSESSMENT

Another best practice is to get feedback from your project team about how the whole project went. This is especially important if you see future projects on the horizon. The best way to do this is to:

☞ Have the project manager use an anonymous survey tool such as www.surveymonkey.com or www.selectsurvey.net to send a questionnaire to the project team members. You can find an example of such a survey in the Helpful Resources section at www.simplyinnovate.net.

☞ Compile the results of this questionnaire, look at any key positives and negatives, and use them as the basis for a one-hour closing meeting that you will host.

☞ At the meeting, thank the team for its efforts, and let the members know that this closing assessment exercise is simply to learn from the process so that the next project will be even better than the project just completed.

☞ Post-meeting, send out a recap of what was learned. This can be sent out more widely in the company if you deem it appropriate.

FAILURE DOES HAPPEN

I would be remiss if we didn't talk about failure, since Chapter 3 talks about how failure is part of innovation. It's worth repeating that failure is part of innovation, and it is OK, as long as the reason the project failed is because you took a calculated risk and not because you failed to follow the process outlined in this book or because you didn't do enough research. Remember all those land mines listed in Chapter 3? It's possible that even with these warnings, one of those land mines could have tripped you up. It happens. I bet you learned a lot from this, and experiences like this are ultimately very positive for your resumé. Good interviewers will ask you to tell them about the time you did something that didn't work out. And talking about a failure is a great thing because of the experience you gained throughout the process.

CELEBRATE

You and your team worked hard. It's time to celebrate your achievement. Even if you failed, you should still celebrate. If you've got a little money to spend, have lunch, make some goofy awards to hand out, and think of some fun memories that your team experienced during the course of the project. Get creative and have fun: Create custom-designed T-shirts, or go to a ball game or bowling. If you don't have any budget to celebrate, then a potluck or dessert in the breakroom one afternoon works. For awards, you can create fun certificates acknowledging the team's contributions.

Part II Action Summary

Chapter 4

- Write down your business challenge.

- Make sure you are solving the right challenge by talking to people and doing some research.

- Use the jobs to be done, outcome expectations, and/or ethnography methods to help you hone in on the biggest business challenge that you will use innovation to solve.

- Revise your business challenge, if necessary.

Chapter 5

- Read and use the "idea generating hints." You may want to print them out or copy them.

- Select at least two to three each of the gathering, borrowing, and observing section ideas, and use them to create a list of possible innovative solutions for your business challenge. Don't limit yourself; you can use as many of these idea-generation methods as you want.

- Let the ideas bounce around in your brain.

- Do some casual and/or formal brainstorming:
  - ➤ Read the brainstorming rules first.
  - ➤ Use a brainstorming session to further the seeds of ideas you gathered from a previous exercise; or, if you don't have many ideas yet, use a brainstorming session to get fresh new ideas.
  - ➤ List any additional ideas you get from a brainstorming session.

Chapter 6

- Decide on your filtering measurements.
- Decide whether to use basic or advanced filtering.
- Get a couple of people to help you filter, if possible.
- Write your ideas down on the filtering form, and evaluate them.
- Total up all the numbers, and see which idea rises to the top.
- If some ideas need further research, do it, and then re-filter.
- Select the best idea that will solve your business challenge!

Chapter 7

- Get an executive sponsor.
- Complete the project charter.
- Complete any additional support that you will need to get approval for this project.
- Get your project approved.
- Put a team together to implement your idea (make sure you have someone with project management skills).

Chapter 8

- Complete the first draft of your project plan (both major and minor steps).
- Hold your first team meeting.
- Follow the six bulletpoint items in the "get the project going" section to make sure your project moves ahead smoothly.
- Make sure you have checkpoints set up to either move forward or kill the project.

Chapter 9

- Test your idea, if possible; adjust, if necessary.
- Roll out our your innovation.
- Get feedback; make any necessary adjustments.
- Monitor post-rollout; make any necessary adjustments.
- Do a post-project assessment with your team.
- Celebrate!

PART III – THE WRAP UP

Now that you are an innovation juggernaut, let's talk about a few things that could help you push an innovation agenda within your company. I like the concept that Jim Collins uses in his book *Good to Great*[3] about the flywheel. It's very hard to get that flywheel moving; there is an incredible amount of strength needed to get it started. However, once you have the flywheel spinning, it's equally hard to stop. You, as one person, can only do so much. But the cool thing is you can do something; just don't give up hope, and don't get frustrated (remember, there are some things you can't control that we discussed in Chapter 2).

Chapter 10: Making a Case for Innovation with Your Company

It's unfortunate but true. There are many more non-innovative companies out there than innovative companies. So what can you do to encourage innovation in your company? I'm glad you asked.

USE YOUR INFLUENCE

Everyone can influence. You influence people multiple times every day through your words and your actions. If you have kids, I don't need to say much more, as you will agree with me that children, especially when young, pick up their parents' habits (good and bad). Think of that person you saw while you were driving who yelled at you for no good reason. They influenced you (they either pissed you off, or you looked after them with a sense of wonder and amusement; either way, you were influenced).

The key to encouraging innovation in your company is to consciously influence. Here are ways you can do this:

- The No. 1 way to influence people around you is to lead by example. Finding an incremental innovation and implementing it successfully is the best way to influence people around you. And, finding ways to communicate this success is important. It's OK to "toot your own horn," especially if you focus on the innovation itself rather than the "I thought of it" aspect.
- Share with your co-workers tidbits you learned from this book and other innovation hints you've picked up along the way. You can turn them onto the Helpful Resources section of www.simplyinnovate.net, which has many helpful items for someone who wants to learn more about innovation.
- If you hear your boss or an executive within your company express an interest in innovation, suggest that he or she read the book that starts right after this one, *Top-Down Innovation*. Hopefully, that person will be so interested they also will read *Bottom-Up Innovation*, which is really important if they become serious about innovation.

- Make a case for innovation in your company if you are in a position to do this and see an opening. This can seem a bit radical, but sometimes you will find an opportunity when your boss or an executive in your company is inquiring about innovation. You can share a PowerPoint with him or her (find one you can build from at www.simplyinnovate.net in the Helpful Resources section). Take this PowerPoint and modify it based on your company's goals and additional research you conduct. If you are not in a position of authority, you may present alongside your boss or that executive whom you talked with.

- If your company has regular employee meetings, suggest to the person who prepares the agenda that they include a short 10-minute discussion about one aspect of innovation. A lot of possible educational tidbits could be discussed. Almost any one of the Helpful Hints sections in this book could be turned into a short innovation presentation with a little bit of effort. Also, if you go to www.simplyinnovavate.net and click on the Media Room tab, you will see a series of short videos titled "Innovation in 66 seconds." These can be shown in the meeting by whomever is leading it. There are also some other cool innovation videos found from across the web in the Media Room.

CHAPTER 11: FINAL CONFESSIONS. TELL ME YOUR STORY!

This book is an innovation in and of itself. Therefore, I want to learn how this book impacted you so I can improve upon future revisions. I can't do this without your honest feedback. I appreciate all your comments. If you had a great success, let me know and I may use your story (with your permission) in my book or on my website. Please go to www.simplyinnovate.net, and use the comments section. You can also email me at feedback@simplyinnovate.net.

Do you enjoy innovating? If so, do the following:

- Read *Top-Down Innovation*. Hey, you already bought it as part of this book. It will give you some great insights into how a company needs to change in order to create a lasting innovation culture.
- Keep learning more about innovation. There are great blogs and other great books out there that focus on specific areas of innovation. See Appendix B for some that I like, and go to the Helpful Resources tab at www.simplyinnovate.net for all kinds of useful links.
- Start with one small incremental innovation, but use the process in this book to do it.
- Keep influencing people around you. Look for those opportunities to influence; they will come up.

Enjoy Work and Life!

You likely spend 40 hours a week at work (some of you spend a lot more). At a minimum, that equals almost 40 percent of your waking hours each week! By adding in commuting and weekday lunch, you likely spend more time at work than you do with your family.

Because of this, life is really too short and precious not to follow these two rules when it comes to work:

☞ Be happy at work and make it fun.

☞ Ensure your work is challenging and interesting.

Innovation can reinvigorate your attitude and work career. However, if despite your best efforts and attitude, you aren't able to live by these two rules, it's time to reflect on your worklife and perhaps think about finding greener pastures. It's just my opinion, but I believe it's worth pondering.

helpfulhints

Part III Action Summary

Chapter 10

🏃 Use your influence to further innovation in your company.

Chapter 11

🏃 Send me feedback about how to improve this book and any success stories at www.simplyinnovate.net.

Bottom-Up Innovation: Websites and Credits

Website References

- ❖ Chapter 2 – You Can't Control the Creativity of People Around You – The Kirton Method: http://www.kaicentre.com
- ❖ Chapter 3 – Competing Projects – The Five Starving Monkey Rules: http://www.informationweek.com/news/208403794
- ❖ Chapter 4 – Jobs to be Done – Clayton Christensen's YouTube video: http://www.youtube.com/watch?v=s9nbTB33hbg&feature=results_video&playnext=1&list=PL48AA1B5D48196765
- ❖ Chapter 4 – Outcome Expectations – Anthony Ulwick's concept: http://www.youtube.com/watch?v=tcGMDnKo-X0&feature=related
- ❖ Chapter 4 – Ethnography – Quicken's "Follow me Home" program: http://www.inc.com/magazine/20040401/25cook.html
- ❖ Chapter 4 – Ethnography – OC Bicycle Service + Garage: http://orangecountybicycleservicegarage.com/home/
- ❖ Chapter 5 – Gathering Ideas – Crowdsourcing: www.innocentive.com
- ❖ Chapter 5 – Where do People Come Up With Their Best Ideas – Dr. Sanjay Gupta video on how sleeping helps you ideate: http://www.youtube.com/watch?v=heM-exrL0Dk
- ❖ Chapter 5 – Observing – Entertaining look at some wacky people: www.peopleofwalmart.com
- ❖ Chapter 8 – Learn More about Project Management – Educational slideshow: http://www.score.org/resources/guide-project-management.
- ❖ Chapter 8 – Learn More about Project Management: http://management.about.com/od/projectmanagement/ht/ProjMgtSteps.htm
- ❖ Chapter 9 – Closing Assessment – Online survey tools: www.surveymonkey.com or www.selectsurvey.net

Credits

1. Dr. Michael Kirton's Adaption-Innovation theory:
   http://www.kaicentre.com
2. Oncken, William Jr., Donald L. Wass, and Stephen R. Covey. Management Time: Who's Got the Monkey? *Harvard Business Review*, November-December 1999: http://hbr.org/product/management-time-who-s-got-the-monkey/an/99609-PDF-ENG
3. Collins, Jim. *Good to Great: Why Some Companies Make the Leap … and Others Don't*. HarperCollins, 2011: http://www.jimcollins.com/books.html
4. Ulwick, Anthony. *What Customers Want: Using Outcome-Driven Innovation to Create Breakthrough Products and Services*. McGraw-Hill Books, 2005: http://www.strategyn.com/resources
5. Christensen, Clayton M., and Michael E. Raynor. *The Innovator's Solution*. Harvard Business School Publishing Corp., 2003: http://www.claytonchristensen.com/books.html
6. Silverstein, David, Philip Samuel, and Neil DeCarlo. *The Innovator's Toolkit: 50+ Techniques for Predictable and Sustainable Organic Growth*. John Wiley & Sons Inc., 2009: http://www.innovatorstoolkit.com
7. Bhidé, Amar V. *The Origin and Evolution of New Businesses*. Oxford University Press, 2000: http://www.bhide.net/origin_index.html
8. Murray, David Kord. *Borrowing Brilliance: The Six Steps to Business Innovation by Building on the Ideas of Others*. Penguin Publishing, 2009: http://www.davidkordmurray.com/books
9. Duggan, William. *Strategic Intuition: The Creative Spark in Human Achievement*. Columbia University Press, 2007: http://www.cup.columbia.edu/book/978-0-231-14268-7/strategic-intuition
10. Bienkowski, Danek. Ten Causes of Project Busts. *Computerworld*, Feb. 13, 1989, p.99.
11. Weiss, Joseph W., and Robert K. Wysocki. 5-Phase Project Management: A Practical Planning & Implementation Guide. Perseus Books, 1992.
12. Portny, Stanley E. *Project Management for Dummies*. Hungry Minds Inc., 2001.

Photo Credits

1. Part I – Freeway photo courtesy of billjacobus1 at
   http://www.flickr.com/photos/billjacobus1/125497895/sizes/z/in/photostream/
2. Chapter 1 – 8 Track Tape courtesy of AlishaV at
   http://www.flickr.com/photos/alishav/3520506875/sizes/o/in/photostream/
3. Chapter 1 - Dogs with glasses courtesy of Pacdog at
   http://www.flickr.com/photos/pacdog/64098298/sizes/z/in/photostream/
4. Chapter 3 - Money courtesy of Andrew Magill at
   http://www.flickr.com/photos/amagill/3367543296/
5. Chapter 3 - Pocket watch courtesy of Teresa Thompson at
   http://www.flickr.com/photos/theresasthompson/2890302952/
6. Chapter 3 -Tiree Perspective courtesy of Nick Jewell at
   http://www.flickr.com/photos/macjewell/2736570618/sizes/l/in/photostream/
7. Chapter 3 - Ice climber Erwan le Lann image at
   http://www.francemag.com/travel-france-travel-articles-france-for-adventure-winter-activities-ice-climbing--108404
8. Chapter 4 - Shell game courtesy of Casablanca PA Blogspot at
   http://casablancapa.blogspot.com/2011/05/shell-game.html
9. Idea dice courtesy of Tnooz Talking Tech Travel site at
   www.tnooz.com
10. Chapter 5 - Word magnets courtesy of Steve A. Johnson at
    http://www.flickr.com/photos/artbystevejohnson/4621636807/
11. Chapter 5 – Piggy Bank IOU courtesy of Jim Corwin at
    http://www.flickr.com/photos/33482346@N05/6267365723/in/photostream/
12. Chapter 7 – Skydiver
13. Chapter 8 – Steps courtesy of ruffin_ready at
    http://www.flickr.com/photos/ryanready/5153564194/sizes/z/in/photostream/

TOP-DOWN
INNOVATION

CREATE AN INNOVATIVE COMPANY!

Table of Contents - Top-Down Innovation

PART I – GUT CHECK

I was a chief financial officer (CFO) and chief administrative officer for a number of mid-sized companies. It was in the position of CFO at the last company for which I worked when I read a survey conducted in 2007 by Futurethink LLC[1] that found that 84 percent of companies surveyed believed innovation was very important for top-line growth, yet only 15 percent of those companies were satisfied with their innovation efforts. As I started to read more about innovation, I realized that my company was leaving real dollars on the table by not making innovation part of our strategic plan.

To make a long story short, I proposed to the board of directors that I lead this effort, and they agreed (with the caveat that I had to backfill my CFO position). I stepped into the role of senior vice president of strategy and innovation, and unlike any position I ever had in the past, I found that not only was there no clear roadmap for what I was supposed to do, there was no GPS, no street signs, not even a road! After years of real-life experience, as well as formal and on-the-job education, I am excited to share with you what I've learned. My goal: to take years of potential frustration and confusion off of your innovation efforts.

Top-Down Innovation not only points out for you the road to innovation, it is your GPS loaded with the latest maps. If you truly want to create an innovative company, this book will show you how to do it. It is a great starting point for innovation; however, you may need other resources as you travel down this road, and I'll tell you where you can find them.

Chapter 1: Can You Benefit from Lasting Innovation?

INNOVATION DEFINED

Let's spend a minute to make sure we are speaking the same language when it comes to innovation. (FYI: If you already read Chapter 1 in *Bottom-Up Innovation,* this little section, and this section only, is the same.)

Innovation is: coming up with *and* implementing ideas that solve some sort of problem or challenge. I invite you to go to my website at www.simplyinnovate.net and click on the graphics on the home page (with the short videos that accompany them) that walk you through the four steps of innovation: identify, ideate, filter, and finish. It's a quick little overview in advance of some of the actionable details coming up in later chapters.

You may have heard different "innovation" terms thrown around, like sustaining, significant, incremental, radical, disruptive, or breakthrough. It's true that some innovations are more radical than others; after all, everyone knows that mp3 players killed CD players, which took out cassette tapes, which threw 8-track players under the bus, which made records obsolete. Those were all pretty disruptive changes (and expensive changes for consumers). But fewer people think about how incremental innovation, like Cascade detergent changing from powder to liquid to self-contained little pouches that combine powder with liquid cleaning agents, can provide a better benefit to their customers and improve a company's profits. Incremental innovations are more common and are important because they can be very profitable.

Incremental Innovation

Once again, when people hear the word innovation, they tend to gravitate to new products, like the iPod. But innovation can come in the form of new processes, or even a brand new business model. For instance, a seemingly minor innovation is being able to deposit checks in an ATM machine without using an envelope. But, while minor, this change saved banks millions of dollars in envelope costs and labor expenses, as well as increased customer satisfaction. (I love it because I don't have to fill out a deposit form, it's quicker and less work, and I get a scanned copy of the check on my receipt.) This innovation wasn't exciting or sexy, but it was innovative.

TOP-DOWN INNOVATION – THE THREE PARTS

Top-Down Innovation is broken into three parts: Part I, which you are reading now, is your gut check. It gives you the background needed for the rest of the book, and importantly, helps you evaluate your company from an innovation standpoint. Part II is your step-by-step guide to building a lasting innovation environment within your company. Part III gives you a few other things to think about to help you achieve long-term innovation success, and it includes tips to help you avoid many of the issues company executives face that can derail innovation.

Along the way, you'll see some words of advice that are especially meaningful in a shaded "Helpful Hints" box like the one below.

Helpful Hint from the Master Thinker

We can't solve problems by using the same kind of thinking as when we created them. — Albert Einstein

---

LET'S LOOK DEEP INTO THE SOUL OF YOUR COMPANY

So let's find out a little bit about your company. Here's a little quiz to start:

- Does your company have some kind of system for capturing ideas from its employees?
- Does your company communicate with employees (including providing educational opportunities) about the importance of innovation?
- Does your company make time available for employees to explore their own ideas?
- Are there controls and processes in place to make innovation a steady stream?
- Does your company have a formal process for selecting which projects to work on, including projects that relate to new innovations?
- Does your company use brainstorming or other methods for generating and developing ideas?
- Does each special project that exists today in your company start with a project charter that identifies the project's objectives and the measurements of success?

OK, let's take a break here. Did you answer "no" to any of the above? The more "nos" you answered, the less innovation appears to be a true priority at your company. Let's ask a couple more questions. If your company does not innovate or does not have special projects that are not part of the normal course of business, then you can skip these questions:

- ➢ Do some of your project or innovation successes happen by chance or luck more than by planning and process?
- ➢ Are the results of your innovation efforts or special projects just OK? Is the value they create not a "Wow!"?
- ➢ Do your innovation efforts ebb and flow depending on the time of year or maybe because there are more important fires to deal with?

If you answered "yes" to any of the above, that further reinforces that you need innovation help.

WHAT'S KEEPING YOU FROM TRULY INNOVATING?

Now that you've looked into the soul of your company, let's try to figure out if there is something terribly dark and deep that is keeping you from innovating.

Chapter 3 in *Bottom-Up Innovation* is the complement chapter to this one. It looks at this question from a non-executive employee's perspective. The perspective at the executive level is a little different. I am making the assumption that you can control (or at least strongly influence) what happens in your company. However, unless you are the president, there may be a few things that you can't completely control. Let's go over some of the more important things that can stand in the way of innovation:

Your CEO Is Not an Innovation Lover

Issue –

This challenge exists in many companies. The head of your company may have a very valid (and long) list of things he or she believes need to be addressed in your company, and adding the rather extensive tasks of building an innovation environment is not one of them. A related issue is that some CEOs can be great at managing short-term tactics, but they are not focused on longer-term strategic issues.

Solution –

Sorry, I don't have a solution for this one. I hate to tell you that building a truly innovative company may not be in the cards right now. If you don't have the support from the top, then it's not likely to happen. I don't want to dash your hopes, but you need to be realistic.

Now the good news: There are things you can do to benefit from innovation, but you are not likely to create an innovation culture that is embedded in all your employees. As we go through this book, I'll tell you what you can still do even if you have this short-term challenge. You will also definitely want to read *Bottom-Up Innovation*, since that book is designed for people who want to innovate in a non-innovative company.

Short-Term Perspective

Issue –

Is your company feeling pressure to deliver short-term results? If you answered yes, there could be a few reasons. If your company has publicly traded stock, you could be pressured to meet the outside analyst's quarterly forecasts. If a private equity firm owns your company, you could be pressured to increase the company's value in time to meet the owner's timeline for selling it. You also may report to (or be) a president who is extremely action-oriented and who wants results now and is less likely to spend effort on projects that may have only a long-term benefit.

Solution –

If you are subject to a lot of short-term pressures, and you don't really care about doing anything that may take a year (or two or three) to show lasting results, then you have the same problem as the previous issue: Building a truly innovative company may not be in the cards right now.

However, if you believe that you can combine some short-term innovations that will deliver some quick profits, along with the task of building a long-term innovation culture, you can try to sell these distinct efforts as a combined package (where some of the short-term innovation projects' profits can help fund the long-term initiatives).

No Tolerance for Failure

Issue –

A key part of an innovation culture is to accept failure as part of the risk-taking process that accompanies innovation. If your company does not tolerate failure, you've got an issue that may severely hinder creating an innovation environment.

Solution –

This is a solvable issue if you have the support from the entire executive team. But, don't expect the environment to change immediately. There will be quite a bit of distrust and disbelief that, all of a sudden, failure (for the right reasons) is OK and is actually expected. This is a long-term change, and we'll discuss this later in more detail.

Money

Issue –

The almighty dollar is definitely one of the key issues. If your company is similar to most larger companies, you have a budgeting process that keeps pretty tight rein on the wallet. If you want to create a lasting innovation environment, in addition to spending money to support great ideas that surface, you will need to spend money building your innovation infrastructure. The challenge is that the money spent on the innovation infrastructure will not have a clearly defined return on investment.

Solution –

One way or another, you're going to need money to innovate. We'll talk about how much you'll need for the various initiatives as we go through this book. If you want to start innovating now, but the budget for the year is set (and not adjustable), you can start with some of the planning, research, and education parts of innovation. Then, when the budgeting process starts for the next year, you'll be in a position to more clearly identify, request, and support money that you want to spend on innovation.

Competing Projects

Issue –

Many companies have a lot of projects (usually too many) hanging around. A common reason for this is that there is no approval or screening process for projects. Sometimes, there is no one making sure a project fits within the strategic plan for the company (and/or the company doesn't even have a strategic plan). Another issue may be that projects don't have any structure around them, so there are no deadlines or measurements that determine success.

Solution –

This is also solvable. We will definitely get into this in detail as we go through this book.

People

Issue –

You need someone at a high level to lead the innovation initiative. You also need one or more people with solid project management skills (which may be different from project leadership skills). And, you need to identify the different creative personality types that exist in your company.

Solution –

This is also solvable, as long as you can solve the money issue. We will get into this in detail as we go through this book.

Chapter 2: The Four Parts of an Innovation Environment

This is a perfect place for a short overview of what you will need to address to create a lasting innovation environment. I am going to break this effort into four important parts and discuss each. These four parts are culture, ideas, roadmap, and structure. Many companies fall into the trap of working on items that are easier than others. This means that many companies are likely to focus their efforts on culture and ideas and put minimal effort into the innovation roadmap and structure.

Culture and ideas are easier to work on because:

➤ Results can be seen relatively quickly.
➤ They don't need the same level of executive leadership.
➤ They are the "sexier" and more visible parts of innovation.

Roadmap and structure are ignored because:

➤ They take many months and even years to see the impact.
➤ They don't have an easily measurable return on investment.
➤ They need senior leaders to drive them.

Also, I mentioned earlier that you might have an issue (or two) that is going to prevent you from building a lasting innovation environment. If so, I am going to give you some special directions.

Look for this symbol, , which I will explain the use of in Chapter 3.

Why Small and Mid-Sized Companies Are In the "Innovation Black Hole"

Why are small and mid-sized companies the worst at innovating?

If yours is a small business, you tend to be pretty innovative, primarily because it's a matter of survival. Many small businesses often fail, though, because they don't offer anything newer than the larger companies they compete with. Conversely, some of the larger companies tend to have whole departments dedicated to innovation. Lockheed's Skunk Works,[2] P&G's Innovation Labs,[3] and Coca Cola's Innovation Lab[4] all are great examples of this.

Mid-sized companies tend to lose the entrepreneurial, innovative spirit that they used to have when they were smaller. They also usually don't have resources dedicated to innovation. Their innovation potential can easily be sucked into the black hole of space. Whatever size company you work for, let's create that innovation environment!

helpfulhints

INNOVATION ROADMAP – YOUR TREASURE MAP

Why do you need to plan? Without a clear innovation roadmap, a company runs into a number of issues. First, it becomes really difficult for the employees to understand how your innovation strategy meshes with your company's overall strategic plan. Next, your innovation efforts lack direction, and you may find out that your time and money were not spent on the most important things.

A good innovation roadmap answers these questions:

- Who owns innovation?
- What will it do for your business?
- How does it complement your overall strategic plan?
- How do you define innovation?
- How will you measure your innovation efforts?

STRUCTURE IS NOT A DIRTY WORD

Structure is the virtual building in which your innovation environment lives. Without this structure, innovators will be exposed to the elements, and they will suffer from sunburn, hypothermia, and windburn.

A clearly defined and universally used innovation structure is critical to your innovation success. Lack of a clearly communicated and consistently managed structure may be the primary reason that companies trying to create a lasting innovation environment fail.

A solid innovation structure includes the following:

- Guidance to help decide where to focus your innovation efforts
- A method for gathering ideas
- Well-designed filters
- A monitoring system that keeps too many projects from choking up your innovation pipeline
- Requirements for the implementation phase of the innovation process
- The tools and resources available at the right time during the innovative idea's lifecycle

CULTURE TAKES TIME

If structure is your innovation backbone, then culture is the soul of your innovative efforts. Without a soul, your innovative efforts will have no desire, no feelings, no will, and no staying power. I don't know about you, but innovation culture sounds very mysterious and nebulous. Let me break it down for you. Some of the elements of an innovation culture include:

- Regular innovation education; this includes general education and skill development for specific individuals necessary for the different parts of the innovation process
- Testing, recognizing, and appreciating different types of creativity
- Creating a physical environment conducive to innovation (e.g., lots of "running into each other" spaces)
- Rewarding and recognizing idea contributors
- Improving access to information
- Creating an atmosphere of transparency and trust
- Celebrating failures, in addition to successes
- Integrating innovation into the strategic planning process
- Creating a separate group and place for innovation, if necessary
- Clearly communicating the organization's innovation roadmap, goals, and processes
- Making sure you have top management buy-in

IDEAS! IDEAS! IDEAS!

Coming up with great ideas is the core of innovation. But even the creative people in your organization can benefit from learning how to ideate and brainstorm with other people. A key part of successful innovating is making sure that your ideas are targeted at solving a specific challenge that relates to your business goals and strategic plan. What's really cool is that there is some great software out there that facilitates the capture of ideas from employees, vendors, and customers, as well as engages these groups to submit ideas and like, comment, and build on other people's ideas.

FOUR CONCEPTS THAT CAN'T LIVE WITHOUT EACH OTHER

After reading through the four parts of building a lasting innovation environment, you probably sensed that there are many interrelationships between these four parts. If you did, you are absolutely correct. That's why it's not going to be nearly as effective if you ignore any of them. 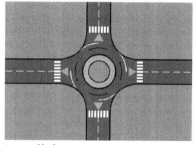 Can you still innovate without addressing all four parts? Sure. But you will suffer from some of the issues mentioned in Chapter 1.

How to Boost Your Creativity

Do you want to find 20 ways to increase your creativity? Check out these tips from About.com Psychology at the link listed in the Website References at the end of this book. There's also some very cool creativity exercises compiled by Michael Michalko at his Creative Thinking website.

Chapter 3: Are You Ready to Commit?

 All right, you have enough information at this point to make a decision. Are you ready to commit to creating a lasting innovation environment? Wait, don't answer yet. I want to be extra sure you know what you are getting into. Remember, you have to be ready to:

- Designate a person in power to lead your innovation efforts (ideally dedicated only to this).
- Plan to spend money (some of it with no immediate return) on innovation.
- Make time for people to innovate (this may mean hiring some people or shifting responsibilities).
- Spend the time to educate and develop skills.

OK, now choose one from the following:

1. Yes, I want to create a lasting innovation environment. I know it's going to take a lot of time, effort, and money, but I really believe it will create some fantastic new successes for my company.
2. No, it's not going to fly. My company flat out doesn't have the time, money, or desire to do this (or, we're doing well and don't need this extra work right now).
3. I would really like to create a lasting innovation culture, but I know that we can't do it right now because of one of the limiting factors discussed in Chapter 1. I do believe we can benefit from innovation by doing some of the things in this book that don't require a company-wide commitment.

Which one did you choose? If you chose number two, it's pretty easy for you. I welcome you to read the rest of the book, because you never know when things might change and you can revisit innovation. But the new season of American Idol might be on, and you would rather watch that.

If you chose number one, congratulations on making that big commitment! I know you may not be fully committed just yet, but you want to read the rest of the book to fully understand what you're getting into. That makes a lot of sense.

If you picked number three, I commend you on being realistic. You're not ready to fly yet, but you're willing to spend some time driving forward with some innovation efforts in spite of the fact that your company as a whole is not ready to innovate. As you continue reading this book, look for sections especially for you, the

Innovation Driver, denoted with this symbol: .

Part I Action Summary

Chapter 1

 Read and enjoy!

Chapter 2

 Read and memorize!

Chapter 3

 Make a commitment. This is important. Be realistic. (Hopefully, it's not number two.)

PART II – LET'S MOVE FORWARD

The meat of this book is going to be in the next four chapters. In these, the innovation roadmap, structure, culture, and ideas concepts will be broken down into manageable bite-sized pieces. When you are in the structure and ideas chapters, I will refer you at times to the *Bottom-Up Innovation* book because it contains a lot of actionable details for these two areas. The nice thing is that *Bottom-Up Innovation* is right in your hands.

Because some of your efforts to establish a structure around your innovation process, culture, and ideas areas can cost money, you might want to spread your efforts out over a period of time if budget is an issue. I'll use the **$** symbol to highlight those actions that will cost some money to implement.

What Are TRIZ and Six Sigma?

TRIZ[5] is a Russian technology for innovating and developing creative ideas for problem solving. TRIZ provides a systematic way of finding solutions, instead of using a trial-and-error method. So, ultimately, it takes less time to solve problems, and results are in the form of more innovative products. TRIZ was originally invented to focus on manufacturing-related problems, but different experts are using it to formulate service-related problems, production problems, etc.

Six Sigma[6] is a business management strategy originally developed by Motorola USA in 1986. It seeks to improve the quality of process outputs by identifying and removing the causes of defects or errors and minimizing variability in manufacturing and business processes.

In recent years, a related concept named Lean Six Sigma formed, which combines Six Sigma ideas with lean manufacturing. The Lean Six Sigma methodology is aimed at promoting business and operational excellence. Companies such as IBM use Lean Six Sigma to focus transformation efforts not just on efficiency but also on growth, serving as a foundation for innovation throughout the organization.

The more complex your business challenge, the more you may benefit from one of these methods. You will need outside experts to help you with these, and you'll need a healthy budget for their help.

helpful hints

Chapter 4: Innovation Roadmap – Your Treasure Map

Have you ever devised a strategic plan? Unless you are the CEO or CFO of a company, you may have seen a strategic plan, but you may have never been responsible for putting one together. In this section we're going to create an innovation version of a strategic plan. I like to call it your innovation roadmap. To make it easy, we are going to put it together one piece at a time.

Strategic plans usually have the following sections:

- Introduction
- Table of contents
- Executive summary
- Background and history
- Strategic action plan focus by year (for three to five years)

Your innovation roadmap should have all of the above sections, in addition to the sections discussed below.

I have created a template for you to use to fill out your innovation roadmap. Go to www.simplyinnovate.net and look under the Helpful Resources tab.

Driver Tip - Since you are only looking for short-term innovation gains, you don't need to put together an innovation roadmap. However, I would suggest you read through this chapter and look out for the symbol for sections that you *do* need to take into account.

DEFINE INNOVATION

While this is pretty basic, you want to make sure everyone in the company is defining definition the same way. Go to Chapter 1 to read a good definition. For your purposes, you want to think about the different types of innovation (incremental vs. significant vs. disruptive).

ALIGN WITH YOUR COMPANY'S STRATEGIC PLAN

Does your company have a strategic plan? If so, you really need to get a copy of the plan to make sure your innovation roadmap is aligned with it.

If your company has a strategic plan, it should include the mission, vision, corporate values, goals, and SWOT (strengths, weaknesses, opportunities, and threats) sections. A strategic plan also usually includes a five-year forecast (although this may exist as a separate document). A strong alignment between your innovation roadmap and your company's strategic plan increases your odds of innovation success.

If your company does not have a strategic plan, then you'll have to do a little more work. See the Helpful Hint below for what you'll need to do.

No Strategic Plan or Mission or Vision?

If your company doesn't have a strategic plan (or a mission or vision statement), then you need to talk to your fellow executives and CEO about what role innovation plays in your company. Usually the reasons people innovate are to drive new sales, reduce costs, address competitive issues, improve a process, improve employee retention/involvement, or solve some other business challenge. Your innovation mission may have elements of one or more of these in it.

WHY INNOVATE? WHAT IS YOUR INNOVATION MISSION?

Creating an innovation mission statement is a good starting point. This statement is your eloquent way of answering: Why do you want to create an innovation environment?

If your company has a mission (and vision) statement, your innovation mission statement likely supports them. For example, part of GM's[7] vision statement is: *"GM's vision is to be the world leader in transportation products and related services. We will earn our customers' enthusiasm through continuous improvement driven by the integrity, teamwork, and innovation of GM people."*

This makes it easy to understand why innovation is important to GM. Let's pick a slightly harder one. Coca Cola's[8] mission statement is: *"To refresh the world... To inspire moments of optimism and happiness... To create value and make a difference."*

So why would innovation be important to Coca Cola? Here's my example of what their innovation mission statement might be: "As the world continues to evolve and new generations adopt different tastes and generational traits, Coca Cola's innovation efforts will deliver new products and delivery systems to meet these new customer needs."

INNOVATION GOALS

Goals are the destination on your innovation trip. Goals are used to bring people together so that they are heading toward the same place. Usually you'll have two to four goals. As you look at all the things you need to do to create a lasting innovation environment, there's a lot to pick from to create your goals. I would suggest you keep going through this book, and as you see things that are important and that strike a chord, write them down as possible goals in the template I provided for you at www.simplyinnovate.net.

Your innovation goals should be SMART (specific, measurable, agreed-upon, realistic, and time-based). I like to emphasize the realistic part of SMART. Don't bite off more than you can chew. You can always create a new set of goals next year after you accomplish this first set.

SWOT – SCAN THE ENVIRONMENT

In this section, you will spend some time assessing and documenting the environment you will be innovating in. SWOT refers to strengths, weaknesses, opportunities, and threats. Most strategic plans will include these four parts, which I prefer. You may want to break them down even further and complete these four parts separately for your internal environment (inside your company) and your external environment (customers/potential customers and industry/competition). It sounds like a lot, but by doing this, it could lead you to an incredibly important part of innovation: a really dialed-in idea of what problem or challenge you are trying to solve with your innovation efforts.

INNOVATION ORGANIZATION

In your strategic plan, you want to talk about people and places. These include:

➢ Innovation leader $ — First and most important, you need a dedicated leader of your innovation efforts. Hiring an innovation leader can be an issue for many companies, because this person is going to command a fairly sizable salary. This person has to be pretty high up in the executive ladder, because he or she has to align his or her decisions with the executive decisions being made, and he or she has to have the power and experience to be able to effect significant change at your company. This person is usually given the title of CIO (chief innovation officer) or its equivalent. When I moved into the role of senior vice president of strategy and innovation, I gave up almost all my CFO responsibilities, but I still oversaw the company's IT and development departments. Fortunately, these departments were headed by two very competent self-managed vice presidents, so I was able to devote most of my time toward my innovation role. There is an incredible amount of work in the beginning when setting up an innovation environment, so don't sell yourself short in this area.

➢ Innovation analyst $ – A lot of set up, research, and monitoring will be required, some of which is not the best use of your CIO's time. The innovation analyst needs to be someone who doesn't mind doing a fair amount of mundane work, as well as someone who helps you put together programs and conduct research and analysis.

➢ Project management skills – Read more about what is a very common issue with many companies in Chapter 7 of the *Bottom-Up Innovation* book's team section.

➢ Time – If your company is like most, you and your fellow employees are pretty darn busy. There are also usually a host of projects going on that take even more of your time. Therefore, you'll need to figure out how you are going to make time for innovation. It is possible, and it will be discussed further in Chapter 6.

➤ Space – Ask yourself: $

  ➤ Can you consider having a completely separate office space dedicated for your innovation group? The sad reality is that this is not feasible in most small companies nor in many mid-sized companies. But consider this: The predominant environment in most companies is not only non-innovative, it can be downright hostile toward innovation, and it will try to kill it like white blood cells killing a virus.

  ➤ Is your current office space conducive toward innovation?

Remember your answer to these questions. They will become important as we delve into space when we talk about your innovation culture in Chapter 6.

HOW WILL YOU MEASURE YOUR INNOVATION RESULTS?

This is an interesting, but important question. There are actually quite a few ways to measure your innovation efforts. They can be measured on ideas submitted, on ideas approved for implementation, or on a number of new innovations that were successfully implemented. Ultimately, your innovations either need to be profitable in their own right (by increasing sales, reducing costs, and/or increasing efficiency), or they need to create an environment that fosters innovations that benefit the company. I usually separate innovation measurement into two pieces: achievement related to creating the long-term innovation environment (which usually has some costs but not an easily quantifiable return) and measurement of specific innovation projects (which had their own project charter and return on investment calculations).

EXPECTED RESOURCE NEEDS SUMMARY

It will be helpful if you recap some of the expected costs to create an innovation culture. After all, you don't want any surprises. However, you might want to save this section until you get through the rest of this section, as you will get a sense for the other items you may need to put in place (e.g., idea software).

Chapter 5: Structure Is Not a Dirty Word

You may think I'm weird when I tell you that structure can be the most exciting part of creating an innovation environment. When you have a clearly defined but simple innovation structure in place, it's cool to see how much it helps not only your innovation efforts, but how much it helps your employees to be more efficient and productive when handling "everyday" projects.

Let's define the innovation structure. Most of the literature about innovation includes some variation of the following four steps, but I prefer these for their simplicity and logic:

☞ Identify (decide upon the challenge that needs innovating)
☞ Ideate (come up with ideas)
☞ Filter (select the best idea)
☞ Finish (turn your idea into a success!)

Part II (Chapters 4 through 9) of *Bottom-Up Innovation* delves deeply into these four steps from the perspective of the employees doing the innovating. Although there is some overlap, the discussion about these four steps in *Top-Down Innovation* focuses on what infrastructure needs to be put into place to ensure that employees can follow the guidance in *Bottom-Up Innovation* without getting their innovation efforts shot down. I highly recommend you read *all* of *Bottom-Up Innovation*, but Chapters 4 through 9 are a must-read (in fact, it's best if you read them right now, and then come back to this page after you are done).

OK, you're back!! Let's walk through the innovation structure.

Driver Tip - If you want to innovate despite the fact that you don't have the company's commitment or a lot of resources, it's not necessary to put a formal process into place. However, there are pieces of this formal process you can apply to your innovation effort. Look for next to the sections that can help you to do this.

Does Structure Slow You Down?

Do you know anybody in your company who is very action-oriented? They may be so action-oriented that they fall into the "ready, fire, aim" category. Or, they may assemble the troops to take the nearest hill, only to be asked afterward: "Was that the right hill to attack?" Many of these "high-urgency" types think that "structure" is a dirty word. It just gets in the way of achievement and dramatically slows things down. It's true that it can. However, a good innovation structure should help clear the road of obstacles and speed up innovation. Just as important, an innovation structure helps make sure that the project is successful, thereby avoiding a massive waste of time or loss of profits if the project were to fail. The goals of the CIO are to create a structure that is *simple but effective*, as well as to communicate the benefits of the structure to these "high-urgency" types.

helpful**hints**

WHO OWNS THE STRUCTURE?

Ideally, the CIO is in charge of putting the structure described below into place. If that person is not on board, you need someone who is detail-oriented, who has authority, who is well-known and respected by the employees, and who is action-oriented. Oh, and by the way, make sure that person has some time on his or her hands.

START BUILDING YOUR STRUCTURE – IDENTIFY THE CHALLENGE

Is your product line going obsolete? Are your retail locations being shut down because of Internet sales? Is your production process too expensive? Is your employee turnover too high? These are all challenges that could benefit from innovation.

The benefit to a company from going through an annual strategic planning process and, thus, creating a strategic planning document, is that it will likely help executives to see what is happening in their business, with their competitors, in the industry, and in the economy in general. Usually, it will help to identify challenges (weaknesses and/or threats).

If this document exists and an innovation roadmap is put into place, you probably have identified one or more business challenges against which to apply your innovation efforts.

The best kind of business challenge is similar to that of a great goal. It must be very specific and measurable. For example: "We want to make our frozen product production line run 40 percent faster while using 20 percent less labor." Or: "We want to increase international sales of our ¼-inch bolts by 35 percent within 18 months without a reduction in price."

However, this is not always the case. You may have what I call "unidentified challenges." This is when you either:

➢ Only have a general sense of what your biggest business challenge is, or
➢ You don't have any idea whatsoever.

If you have a general sense of what your challenge is, but you need some help refining it, then I recommend you use the information in Chapter 4 of *Bottom-Up Innovation* to give you some confidence about whether you have identified the right challenge.

If you have no idea whatsoever what your business challenge is, then my guess is that you don't have an annual strategic planning session. It is probably a good idea for you and the management team to have an ad hoc planning session, in which you take a look at the company and its environment, perform a SWOT analysis, and see if you can identify what your top business challenges are. You also can use some of the tips and tools in Chapter 4 of *Bottom-Up Innovation* to help you.

THE NEXT PHASE OF BUILDING YOUR STRUCTURE – COLLECTING IDEAS

Although we will talk more in depth about the idea phase of structure building in Chapter 7, we'll talk here a bit about the structure to support ideas. In the old days, this was how we collected ideas.

Well, maybe it's not that old. I found this picture on the Office Depot website for $68.99 (free shipping).

The next evolution was to use email to send out requests for ideas. This is a good no-cost solution, but the problem with email is that it is difficult to truly engage people in brainstorming ideas.

Now, we are fortunate to be able to take advantage of new technology that not only collects ideas, but also allows people to "like" ideas and to comment and build on ideas of others. Software like Spigit and Brightidea are relatively affordable and great for idea collection. The larger the company you work in, the more this software will come in handy. **$**

A very important part of idea gathering is to issue a specific challenge (that's why you need to perform the first step in this chapter to identify your challenge). Research has shown that the most effective idea-gathering campaigns are ones that are challenge-based and only open for a limited period of time (e.g., two weeks)

 EVALUATION TEAM – STAGE 1 OF FILTERING

So you have your business challenge, and you asked for ideas and gathered them. Now, what do you do with them? Put together an evaluation team — a diverse group of employees at different levels and from different departments. Look for employees who want to be part of this team and who aren't afraid to speak their mind, even in front of executives. A group of five to seven employees is perfect. The team should rotate every six months to a year, and it should have criteria to use when evaluating ideas. For more information on filtering, see Chapter 6 of *Bottom-Up Innovation*. You can download filtering templates from the Helpful Resources section at www.simplyinnovate.net.

The evaluation team will do one of three things with ideas:

- Accept them.
- Reject them.
- Assign the idea to one or more of the team members for further analysis and to resubmit for evaluation.

In a perfect environment, the best idea to solve a specific business challenge will be the one that rises to the top. But it's OK if you end up with a few great potential ideas (innovations) that can address your business challenge. These ideas will be submitted to the screening committee for a final decision.

SCREENING COMMITTEE – STAGE 2 OF FILTERING

The screening committee is different from the evaluation team. The only person who should be on both teams is the CIO. The screening committee should consist primarily of members of the executive team. This is important. You want the buy-in of this group because money and resources are going to be needed for any idea that is approved.

Before the idea comes in front of the screening committee, some work needs to be done. The evaluation team will appoint one of its members to sponsor the idea, and the idea will be given to a selected group of employees that is best suited to complete the following for the idea:

➤ Summary of idea
➤ Project charter
➤ Return-on-investment detail
➤ Summary of your filtering efforts

The screening committee will do one of three things with the idea:

➤ Accept it.
➤ Reject it.
➤ Send the idea back to be reworked (this means that more information is needed).

If multiple ideas for the same challenge were submitted, only one potential innovation should survive the screening committee's review.

Bad Filtering Methods

Keep an eye out for the following bad filtering methods that are used to select projects:

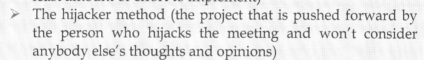

- ➤ The CEO method (the project that the CEO likes)
- ➤ The CFO method (the project that costs the least)
- ➤ The couch potato method (the project that takes the least amount of effort to implement)
- ➤ The hijacker method (the project that is pushed forward by the person who hijacks the meeting and won't consider anybody else's thoughts and opinions)

These methods tend to pop up in companies that don't have a clear structure in place. Even though they can be humorous, they actually happen quite a lot.

helpfulhints

PIPELINE MANAGEMENT, VISIBILITY, AND COMMUNICATION

What's in your basket?

We talked earlier about different levels of innovation (incremental, significant, disruptive) and different types of innovation (new products or services, new business process, a whole new line of business, etc.). The larger the company, the more different types of innovation efforts you should have in your innovation pipeline. Ideally, you don't want all your innovation efforts to be one type or one level. For example, if you have a number of innovation efforts that are all disruptive or radical, these usually take a very high level of effort and are more risky than incremental or significant innovations. A great analogy can be made using your retirement investments. The standard advice is that it is best to diversify in stock, bonds, money market funds, etc. The same is true for your innovation efforts. The CIO should monitor this pipeline using some of the methods discussed below.

Visibility and communication: What are we working on?

This is actually part of communications, which is the next little sub-section. How do you make the details of your innovation efforts available to not only the team working on it but all your employees?

Team members should be able to access all the documents related to the innovation project in one place. The options I have used include creating a special Microsoft Outlook folder on the company server that is accessible to only team members; Google docs, which is very helpful if you have outside partners working with you on the project; and the company intranet using Microsoft SharePoint to create a custom innovation project section.$ While this last option worked well, we did not have our SharePoint site configured to allow outside partners to view this section (although it can be configured to allow outside people in).

You may question the idea of letting all employees know what innovations you are working on. It's a valid question. Depending on what the innovation is, you may want to shroud your efforts in secrecy because you don't want the news to leak outside of your company (and the more employees who know about it, the more likely a leak may occur). The flip side of this is that the more you can communicate about your innovation efforts, the more you will influence the culture of your company. If you have a company intranet, this is a great place to create an innovation page that you can update regularly. Once again, I have successfully used Microsoft SharePoint for this, but any intranet can work. Do you hold regular employee meetings, put out company newsletters, have a monthly president's message or some other regular communication? These are all great venues to add some news on the status of your innovation efforts. If you don't do any of these, your project leader can work with the CIO, public relations, or marketing person to put out a quarterly communication, even if it just an email.

Kill the Starving Monkeys

I know, it sounds terrible. But I'm not asking you to harm any wildlife. In addition to monitoring the innovation pipeline, your innovation leader should track all the projects going on in your company. Any project that exists has the potential to take away resources from your innovation projects. It's possible a lot of these other projects have never been formally approved, don't have a project charter, are not adequately resourced, and don't have any measurements for success. They are just sort of hanging around in the shadows, getting fed a banana now and then, but slowly starving. These are the "Starving Monkey" projects that need to be knocked off. (Starving Monkey is part of a time-management article written by William Oncken Jr. and Donald Wass for the *Harvard Business Review* in 1974). A very good *Information Week* article gives a nice description of the five rules. A link to this article can be found in the Website References at the end of this book.)

helpfulhints

YOU NEED TOOLS

As part of creating a solid structure to support your innovation efforts, you'll need educational and skill-based resources available to your team. An important part of the CIO or executive sponsor's responsibility is to assess what these needs are prior to a lack of skill or knowledge becoming a problem. A great example of this is a project I sponsored for which the project leader did not have all the skills needed to also be a stellar project manager (see the Project Team section in Chapter 7 of *Bottom-Up Innovation*). Our company had a couple of employees who had great project manager skills, but they were not available. So I hired a project manager from outside the company to consult on this project. It was awesome. She was Six Sigma black belt-certified, had a great personality, and was incredibly organized. Out of the 20 or so meetings that were held during the course of the project, she attended only two of them in person; the others she attended remotely via GoToMeeting. I firmly believe the project would not have gone as smoothly as it did without bringing her on.

Your team also will need the support of innovation tools. Does your project leader know and share the ground rules for the weekly meetings? Does your team know how to hold brainstorming sessions when it runs into issues? Does your team know how to test your innovation effort before it rolls out? The executive sponsor should stay close enough to the project (including attending some of the meetings) to make sure the tools and support are provided. The CIO also should provide some of this support.

TOOLS, TOOLS, AND MORE TOOLS

A number of tools and techniques can be used for each of the four phases of the innovation process (identify, ideate, filter, and finish).

Some can be quite powerful for determining customers' needs and ways to modify your product or service. Others can be great for supporting the idea-generation phase. And some other tools can support the testing and other aspects of the implementation phase.

I recommend the book *The Innovator's Toolkit*[9] by David Silverstein, Philip Samuel, and Neil DeCarlo. It is worth the investment as it lists 50 tools and techniques, tells you step by step how to use them, and lets you know when you may need outside help to use some of the techniques.

helpfulhints

INNOVATION SOFTWARE AND CONSULTANTS WHO DO IT ALL!

I believe that individuals need to know their limitations. You and your fellow employees are probably the cream of the crop: incredibly smart and dedicated. Still, you may not have the right skills or the time to do everything in this book.

There are a lot of smart people who have either developed comprehensive software to help you throughout the entire innovation process and/or they offer consulting services to help you with your innovation efforts. I view these people and companies as great resources, not competitors. However, they can be expensive, so they're not likely to be affordable for the smallest businesses. Go to the Helpful Resources section of www.simplyinnovate.net to find a list of some of these resources. For more in-depth information about their offerings, you will see my comments about them. $

Chapter 6: Culture Takes Time

In Chapter 2, I introduced you to innovation culture. In this chapter, I'm going to delve deeper into the finer points and give you specific actionable advice to start working on changing your company from a staid, stable, complacent company to an energized, creative, dynamic, innovative organization. (I hope I didn't just oversell this chapter.) There are a number of actions you can take with people, space, time, and communications.

Innovation Culture vs. Corporate Culture vs. Brand Culture

Remember in Chapter 2 when I explained the difference between the different types of company culture? As you put together your innovation culture plan, remember that you don't want your efforts to conflict with your corporate culture or brand culture.

For example, if your corporate culture focuses on minimizing failures, then you have a conflict that needs to be resolved among the executive team because failure and innovation go hand in hand.

Driver Tip - If you don't have the commitment to innovate or a lot of resources, but you do *want* to innovate, you don't need to put into place a long-term innovation culture plan. However, I still recommend that you read this entire chapter, and then address those sections that have the little sports car next to them.

CREATE AN INNOVATION CULTURE PLAN AS PART OF YOUR INNOVATION ROADMAP

We talked about creating an innovation roadmap as part of your strategy work in Chapter 4. Part of this roadmap includes creating an innovation culture plan. This part of embedding innovation in your company can take multiple years before substantial changes take place, so plan accordingly, and don't try to do everything at once, as you will quickly become inundated. Read through all the things I describe in this chapter, and then schedule them on a calendar based on what you believe is their order of importance. Some of the items will be ongoing forever, but setting them up and getting them rolling can take a lot more effort than keeping them running.

PEOPLE AND CULTURE $

Creativity: Testing, recognizing, educating, and appreciating

I'm going to ask you to go to the end of Chapter 2 of the *Bottom-Up Innovation* book and read the section titled "You Can't Control the Creativity of People Around You." Now that you've done that, you understand that people tend to fall into one of two personality buckets when it comes to creativity. If you went to the website I referenced and checked out the PowerPoint, you probably can use that information to gauge which bucket the employees you work with fall into. Better yet, use KAI[10] to test your employees. Myers-Briggs[11] is another good tool, which will tell you a lot about what engages your employees, although its methodology differs from KAI. However, if your company already uses a personality test, I wouldn't necessarily recommend spending money to purchase another.

No matter whether you test your employees or not, I would still recommend that you hold educational sessions (either with your project team, by company department, or the entire company), and have the employees self-assess themselves. I did this at a company I worked for. At our quarterly employee meeting, I took 10 minutes out of the agenda to explain the KAI theory and some of the attributes of an adaptor vs. an innovator. Then I distributed pieces of paper and asked the employees to select a style that they felt best represented themselves. I had a couple of people tabulate the results during the rest of the meeting so that by the end, I was able to share the number of adaptors vs. innovators.

Quite a few of employees shared with me afterward what they put on the paper, and based on my observations, I think most of the employees did a good job with their self-analysis. The biggest "Aha!" of this presentation was the realization by the employees that, many times, when they were frustrated by a fellow employee's behavior, this was simply a reflection of their creativity type; the reason they were frustrated is because they were likely the opposite type. I then shared that they should instead appreciate this difference because the strongest teams and companies need both of these types.

That was an eye-opener for many employees, and I saw immediate differences in behavior. Instead of getting frustrated, there was friendly joking about their creative style, which was well-received and sometimes brought that extreme person back to Earth for a little while.

Testing employees can be moderately expensive. But, if you just perform the educational part, it should cost very little.

Innovation Education

The cool thing about innovation education is that there are many low-cost or no-cost ways you can do it. Let's first talk about general (not project- or person-specific) education. The first good news about education is that you have enough material for at least a couple of years of education sessions sitting in your hands. You know all the Helpful Hints sections I have sprinkled throughout this book? Each of those can be a five- to 10-minute mini-education session that you can create as part of your regular company employee meetings. Or, you can create a "lunch and learn" session once a month at which you present a new innovation concept and spring for some cookies after the employees eat their lunch. You don't have to limit yourself to the Helpful Hints boxes. Almost any section of this book can be transformed into an education session. Since educating the general employee base about innovation is a longer-term initiative, it makes sense for you to plan an education series that starts with the basics and builds on more complex subjects over time. Also, if you have high employee turnover, don't assume that what you presented a year ago was seen by everyone you are talking to today. You can solve this issue by having special education sessions for new employees or having an archive of your presentations available. You also can go to www.simplyinnovate.net and click on the "Top Secret Hideaway" tab, where you will find a series of "Innovation in 66 Seconds" videos that you can play for your employees. These are quick, fun, and informative.

If you have or intend to have specific people dedicated to innovation (like your CIO or innovation analyst), they could benefit from individualized education. I attended a great CIO seminar hosted by BMGI (www.bmgi.com). I also attended a very informative conference held by the idea software company Spigit (www.spigit.com). There are a lot of innovation sessions and conferences that would benefit your innovation employees. Expect to spend a fair amount of money for travel and training costs, but it's worth it.

Now let's talk about the training for people on your innovation projects. Does your project leader need team-building skills or meeting management skills? Do you need to train some internal people on project management skills? Do you want your team to be better brainstormers, or do they need organizational skills to better meet deadlines? The project leader, executive sponsor, and CIO all should be involved in assessing the needs of the project team. Then, they should find classes or other resources to educate the team about the skills they need to successfully create and roll out your new innovation. If you have a good human resources and/or training department, they may be able to help you find the educational resources you need.

 Trust & Transparency: Do You Have It?

Does your company environment have any of the following issues?

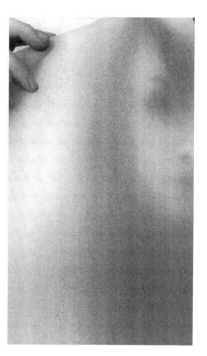

> ➢ Lack of communication
> ➢ A habit of placing blame/pointing fingers at other employees
> ➢ Lack of respect for other employees
> ➢ Frustration and even anger shown by employees
> ➢ Low morale (hopefully measured on a regular basis)
> ➢ Backstabbing (in order to look good to superiors)
> ➢ A feeling of secrecy or "I don't know what's going on"
> ☺ No diet sodas in the vending machine?

Any of the above issues are signs that you have an opportunity to improve the trust between your employees. Higher levels of trust result in increased efficiency of teams and higher productivity throughout the company.

Some of the things you can do to improve trust and transparency are:

☞ Ensure that employees involved in projects possess the skills necessary to successfully contribute to the project.

☞ Ensure that project leaders possess the leadership skills to lead teams both within their function and across functions for company-wide initiatives.

☞ Identify and address obstacles related to lack of trust by:

> ✌ Establishing consistent expectations for project team members.

> ✌ Effectively communicating (training, mentoring, etc.) established expectations throughout the organization.

> ✌ Measuring success of projects and individual team members against established expectations.

Move Your Innovation Culture from Good to Great

Jim Collin's book *Good to Great*[12] has some great words of wisdom that relate to building trust and transparency. "Doing an autopsy without blame," "Confront the brutal facts," and "Build red flags that turn information into information that cannot be ignored" all are great precepts to follow as you work on building trust in your organization.

helpful**hints**

Celebrate Failure!

A key part of an innovation culture is to accept failure as part of the risk-taking process that accompanies innovation. You may work for a company that frowns upon failure. If so, it's going to take a fair amount of effort to turn around that mindset, which may have been ingrained for years and perhaps decades. Depending upon how anti-failure your company is, don't expect this mindset to change in a week, a month, or possibly even a year. It will take time.

Here are some ideas you can use to move toward a culture that accepts failure as an integral part of innovation:

> Educate employees about how failure is part of innovation. Use examples from history. (Thomas Edison is reported to have failed thousands of times before he succeeded with the light bulb.)

> Make sure you communicate that failure happens when you innovate because you take a calculated risk. The more radical the innovation, the higher the risk of failure. I like the term "successful failure" for this kind of failure.

> Communicate (and make sure you have management buy-in on this concept) that when you give people freedom to succeed, you also must give them freedom to fail.

> Clarify that failure is not OK because you didn't do enough research or because you took shortcuts and didn't use the innovation structure in your company. I like to call this "avoidable failure."

> Always make sure you have post-mortem meetings after the project ends so you can learn from both your successes and your failures. (Learn more about this in the "Closing Assessment" section of Chapter 9 of *Bottom-Up Innovation*.)

> Celebrate failures in addition to successes. Every project should have some kind of celebration at the end of the project. You and your team worked hard. It's time to celebrate your achievement. Even if you successfully failed, you still should celebrate. If you've got a little money to spend, have a lunch, make some goofy awards to hand out, and think of some fun memories that your team experienced during the course of the project. If you don't have any budget to celebrate, a potluck or dessert in the break room one afternoon works also. For awards, you can create certificates (that can be fun) acknowledging the team's contributions.

- ➢ Create a failure wall. Jeff Stibel[13] wrote in the _Harvard Business Review_ _Blog Network_ about his efforts to create a company culture in which employees take risks without fear of reprisal. The link to this article can be found in the Website References at the end of this book.
- ☺ Make a sign that says "I'm a Failure," and make the project leader wear the sign around his neck for a week (wait, that's really not funny).

SPACE AND ITS IMPACT ON CULTURE $

Can you consider dedicating a completely separate office space for your innovation group? Having such a space can give you a chance at a cultural "fresh start" with employees who are separated from the potentially non-innovative culture of the rest of the company that you are trying to change.

As we discussed in the "Innovation Organization" section in Chapter 4, the sad reality is that this is not feasible in most small companies and many mid-sized companies. If not, you can do the following to make your existing space more conducive to innovation:

➢ If you have open common spaces, put some comfortable chairs and décor in them (make one feel like a living room). You want it to be accessible and casual. This invites people to sit down, mingle, and brainstorm.
➢ It's also nice if you have a quiet, soothing reflection space (think massage room, complete with the music but without the masseuse).
➢ Another option is a relaxing room for fun and creativity with games and books/videos, funky art, objects like a guitar, etc.
➢ If you are remodeling, think about creating a more open environment with fewer walls and more opportunity to mingle. Also, you can give conference rooms a different feel by placing them where windows are and making them more inviting with smaller tables that can be moved around.

➢ Make sure your existing conference rooms have easels and places where you can post ideas on the walls.

☺ When the CEO is on vacation, turn his office into a recreation room complete with pool table, foosball and a pinball machine (the CEO's office is usually big enough for all this).

Great Read About Creative Spaces

Tom Kelley is the cofounder of a very famous design firm, IDEO. In his book, *The Art of Innovation*,[14] Kelley devotes a chapter about how important having a creative physical environment is to the innovation process and what that looks like at IDEO. The entire book is interesting, but this chapter is very helpful for giving you a good visual of what is possible.

helpful**hints**

TIME AND ITS IMPACT ON CULTURE

Where does time go? In this book, we want your company innovators to identify challenges, conduct research, ideate, evaluate, screen, collaborate, analyze, implement, test, adjust, refine, monitor, communicate, lead, learn, and celebrate. Where are they going to find the time to do all this?

Assuming that you are going to staff your innovation department as described in Chapter 4, follow the lead of some of the most innovative companies that do some cool things to give their employees time to innovate. Here are some examples:

🕐 Google gives its workforce 20 percent of its time to work on projects not immediately connected to its core business.[15]

🕐 3M has a program called "15 Percent Time" that allows employees to use a portion of their paid time to chase rainbows and hatch their own ideas.[16]

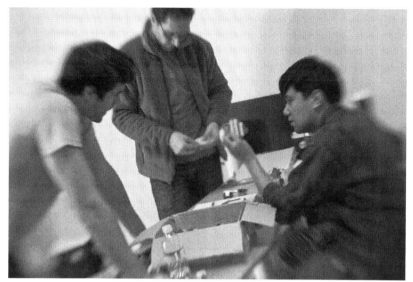

🕐 W.L. Gore, with its program called Dabble Time, gives its workforce a half day each week to follow its fascinations.[17]

🕐 Corel instituted its "Virtual Garage" program that helps the company capture, evaluate, and develop ideas created by its rank-and-file employees.[18]

🕐 Atlassian, a very successful Australia-based software company, has an innovative concept named "FedEx Day," which is a 24-hour innovation immersion event that enables employees to brainstorm, prototype, and pitch their emerging innovations. Each FedEx Day starts at 2 p.m. and ends (with a lot of pizza, beer, and giddiness in between) with a spirited round of presentations delivered 24 hours later. Lots of useful and successful innovations have come out of "FedEx Days" that would not have otherwise been ideated.[19]

Other less-exciting things you can do to create more time for employees are:

🕐 Create a "stop doing" list. It's amazing, when you break down a person's job responsibilities into individual detail, how many things either really don't need to be done, or how much more quickly they can be accomplished.

🕐 When detailing duties, you also will likely find some that can either be temporarily or permanently reassigned, freeing up the employee to be part of an innovation effort.

Time = Ideas = Innovation Success

I've come across the following line a number of times, so I'm not sure who to give credit to (it's not me):

"Remember, organizations do not innovate. *People* do. And people need time to innovate."

helpful hints

COMMUNICATION AND CULTURE

Advice about communication has been sprinkled throughout this book. This is because communication is like the nervous system in your body — deeply intertwined and conscious of the workings of every other system. Below is a summary of the different key communication points:

◀ Clearly communicate the organization's innovation strategy, goals, and structure.

◀ Improve access to information to improve communications throughout the company and within your innovation project teams.

◀ Communicate the risks at

the outset of the project (before it's approved).

◀ Communicate the status of the project on a regular basis as you turn your idea into reality.

◀ Make sure regular communication is occurring between the executive sponsors and their respective project leaders.

◀ Create an innovation structure; it is critical to your innovation success. Lack of a well-built, clearly communicated, and consistently managed structure can prove fatal to your innovation efforts.

◀ Communicate the benefits of this structure to the "high-urgency" types.

◀ Communicate and market your innovation achievements, and build excitement over being involved in innovation. Help the project teams communicate their successes.

◀ Make sure you communicate that failure happens when you innovate because you take a calculated risk.

◀ Communicate (and make sure you have management buy-in on this concept) that when you give people freedom to succeed, you also must give them freedom to fail

Chapter 7: Ideas! Ideas! Ideas!

Think about this scenario: You send an email that says: "We want to come up with some ideas to improve our profits; please email me with your ideas." It's likely you will get some ideas as diverse as "Let's put the lights in our office on motion sensors so they turn off when no one is in the room" to "Let's acquire our competitor." Both of these may be viable ideas (one is a bit more grandiose than the other), but you get the concept that you'll likely get a smattering of ideas.

Don't get me wrong: It's OK to have a comment/idea site where your employees (and others) can post their ideas. Sometimes, you can find nuggets of gold. In fact, mining for gold is a good analogy, since you have to sift through a lot of dirt to find those nuggets. This "open idea box" concept may bring to light problems that hadn't even been identified by management.

What we're going to focus on in this section is different. I'm assuming you've identified a significant business challenge and you are going to share this challenge with your employees and ask them for their ideas. This highly focused, time-limited idea generation campaign keeps you from ending up with an unwieldy mess of ideas.

Your innovation structure outlined in Chapter 5 works essentially the same (from the evaluation team standpoint on) whether you are sifting through the many ideas for that nugget of gold or evaluating ideas that came in as a result of a specific business challenge.

WHERE TO GET IDEAS

The title of this section can be a little confusing. In Chapter 5 of *Bottom-Up Innovation*, I gave a lot of advice about how and where to come up with ideas. You either have read that already, or you will read it shortly. Here, we're talking about the different groups of people to whom you can issue your business challenge in order to solicit ideas.

➢ Your employees are the obvious people to solicit ideas from when you have a business challenge. They are deeply engaged in your business, and they have the best understanding of the products and services you provide.

➢ Next up are your vendors. Most businesses have some vendors with which they have long-standing relationships. Your vendors have the benefit of standing outside of your company and looking in. They may see things that you can't.

➢ If you run a franchise organization, don't forget about these entrepreneurs. Your franchisees have as much or more of a vested interest in your success as you do. Tap into that knowledge base.

➢ Finally, your customers may be a source of ideas for you. We'll talk about the different ways to tap into your customer base, but there are some very useful methods described in Chapters 4 and 5 of *Bottom-Up Innovation* about how to extract information from them.

Get Out! (of the Office)

Get out to:
   ➢ Find out what your customers think and/or what their needs are.
   ➢ Uncover what your competitors are doing.
   ➢ Explore the unknown.
   ➢ Discover new potential customers and opportunities.

Don't stay stuck within those four confining walls. Get out now! Patrick Lefler has a good post about this in the Innovation Excellence[20] blog. Find the link to this blog in the Website References at the end of this book.

helpful hints

HOW TO COLLECT IDEAS $

In Chapter 2, we discussed some of the new software that can help you collect ideas from your employees, vendors, and even customers.

Idea management software effectively puts structure around thoughts. It helps alleviate a historical problem that many companies have: They may have many ideas coming in, but no good means to do anything with them. This kind of software drives ideation more quickly, and it helps you avoid chasing ideas that have already been considered.

Most good idea management software allows users to submit ideas, comment on other ideas, and "like" ideas. The software also includes the ability to collect ideas on a specific challenge for a specific period of time, and then close off the challenge so the evaluation process can begin. Many software packages also let the employees accumulate points for submitting and commenting on ideas for reward and recognition purposes.

In addition to the basic software, there are other features, some of which are bundled with the idea management software and some that have to be purchased separately. These include evaluation tools, software to manage and merge ideas into proposals, proposal development tools, and various social media tools.

No matter what you do, make sure you follow these rules in your idea-collection efforts:

> When issuing the challenge, don't try to limit the ideas that come in related to that challenge; crazy ideas are fine.
> Find a way to thank each contributor. Most idea software offerings have an automatic reply that you can customize to include a "personal-looking" thank you.
> If you have a rewards program, make sure to reward promptly, visibly, and loudly.

➢ Make sure you keep the database of employees current in your software. At a former company I worked at, we linked the idea software into our Outlook email system so that when employees were added or deleted, it was updated in our idea software.

For customers, this idea software can create an online community space where instant and meaningful feedback can easily be captured, ranked, and routed back to your business. You may find it beneficial for capturing ideas related to incremental feature enhancements, general product feedback, and even breakthrough new product ideas. Here are a couple examples of customer-facing idea sites from the Adobe and GE websites. Find the links to these sites in the Website References at the end of this book.

Driver Tip - If you are not going the full "creating an innovation environment" route, then you likely will not get funding to purchase or license idea software. Your best alternative is to use email to solicit ideas. You can still use some of the rules outlined above.

HOW TO ENCOURAGE IDEAS

Three methods have proved effective for encouraging participation in your idea-gathering efforts:

☞ Recognition

☞ Gamification (see definition below) $

☞ Monetary (or equivalent) rewards $

Monetary rewards are listed third because newer research is showing that recognition and gamification can be more powerful motivators to engage your employees (and customers) than monetary rewards.

For recognition to be effective, it has to be genuine and a big deal. Asking someone to appear in front of the entire office to be recognized for their contribution and to be given a plaque or something similar goes a long way toward getting more people involved in the future.

Gamification simply means applying some of the same techniques that game designers use to engage and motivate users. Spigit is an idea management software provider that applies gamification principles to crowdsourcing business improvement ideas from employees. There is a great article that discusses the trend for innovative companies to add gamification to their innovation toolkit. Find the link to this article in the Website References at the end of this book.

Open Your Arms to "Open Innovation"

According to the official definition of open innovation, it is a concept that assumes companies use external ideas and resources, in addition to internal resources, to further their innovation efforts.

I prefer to define it like this: Open innovation assumes that not all the smartest people in the world work for just your company. If you agree, why not go outside of your company and tap into some of those smart people to help you in your innovation efforts? This could be in the form of consultants to help you with project managers, innovation veterans like myself to help mentor your new innovation leaders (yes, that was a plug ☺), vendors and customers to help you ideate, and innovation software companies to help you create efficiencies.

helpfulhints

Part II Action Summary

Chapter 4

🏃 Get the template to create your innovation roadmap at www.simplyinnovate.net. As you go through the steps below, put the applicable information into this roadmap.

🏃 Get a copy of your company's strategic plan (if it exists), and read it. Or,

> ➤ if your company does not have a strategic plan, talk to your fellow executives (see the Helpful Hints box for what to talk about).

🏃 Create an innovation mission statement (make sure it is in alignment with your company's mission and vision).

🏃 Come up with your innovation goals.

🏃 Perform your SWOT analysis.

🏃 Discuss how you are going to staff your innovation department.

🏃 Discuss your project management capabilities (or lack thereof) and how you will get them, if necessary.

🏃 Talk about how you plan to measure innovation.

🏃 Complete the expected resource deeds summary.

🏃 After you complete each of the next three chapters, come back and update your innovation roadmap so you can address what you are going to do from a structure, culture, and idea standpoint.

🏃 After you have done that, complete the innovation roadmap by completing the executive summary, introduction, and other items mentioned in the second paragraph of Chapter 4.

Chapter 5

- Make sure you read Chapters 4 through 9 of *Bottom-Up Innovation*.

- Select your head of innovation (chief innovation officer, senior vice president of innovation, or whatever the title is).

- Find the additional staff for your innovation department (e.g., analyst, etc.).

- Identify your biggest business challenge that you want to innovate around.

- Select and implement idea software. Boy, I make this sound easy, but it's a lot of work going through the assessment, negotiation, contract, implementation, etc. (See also Chapter 7 for guidance on this.)

- Set up the system of reward and recognition related to the collection of ideas (this will depend in part on the software you implement).

- Create an evaluation team. (See also Chapter 7 for guidance on this.)

- Select the evaluation metrics; your idea management software may or may not help you with this.

- Create the screening committee.

- Create a document to show your innovation pipeline and what stage the ideas are in. This seems early to do since you may not have anything in the pipeline, but it's better to think about this now.

- Create an intranet to:
  - ➢ help project teams share documents for specific projects.
  - ➢ communicate what's going on with innovation.

- Determine whether you want to bring in consultants to help you with all this (after reading this list, I wouldn't blame you; just realize it's going to cost you some money).

Chapter 6

- Put together a long-term plan to create an innovation culture; call it your culture plan that will be included in your innovation roadmap.

- Recommend steps to test and educate around people's creative style.

- Put together an education plan for:
  - ➢ specific innovation department individuals
  - ➢ project managers
  - ➢ project leaders
  - ➢ innovation team members
  - ➢ all employees (general innovation knowledge)

- See if your company has conducted an employee survey recently; if so, get a copy, and assess the responses related to trust and transparency.
  - ➢ If no survey exists, talk to the HR department about how to assess (maybe create an ad hoc survey or informal focus groups).
  - ➢ Put together steps to improve the level of trust in your company (work with HR). (See also some of the ideas in Chapter 6.)

- Put together a "celebrate failure" plan. (See also some of the ideas in Chapter 6.)

- Discuss the options to free up time for employees to innovate.

- Discuss any ideas and recommendations you have for creating innovation space.

- Put together a comprehensive communication plan for innovation.

Chapter 7

- Select idea software, and put together a reward and recognition system.

- Put together a longer-range idea plan for how to connect and get ideas and feedback from groups other than your employees (i.e., vendors, customers, franchisees).

- Do some research on gamification, and determine whether it's something you want to use in your innovation efforts.

- Make sure the use of outside resources (open innovation) is discussed in your innovation roadmap.

PART III – OTHER THINGS TO THINK ABOUT

By now you've got a good sense of what is involved with creating a lasting innovation environment. You can go one of two ways at this point.

On one hand, you might be thinking, "Wow, this is a lot of work and I'm not sure I can pull it off." Remember that innovative companies did not just turn on a light switch and become innovative. They spent many years fostering and nurturing an innovative environment by working on the things we covered in the previous chapters. Some the recommended reading in Appendix B will tell you what companies like Pixar, Apple, Whirlpool and Blizzard Entertainment have done to become innovative powerhouses.

So, the other way you can think about all you have to do is to think like a baby learning to walk. Take one small step at a time and keep positive as you head toward your goal.

Chapter 8: Keep the Momentum Going

As you can see, there is lot to do if you want to create a lasting innovation environment – even in its simplest form – in your company. In this chapter, you will find some advice that can help you with those items that can sneak up and try to upset your innovation efforts. These are important to address and/or watch out for to ensure that your innovation sees the light of day.

Driver Tip – Everything in this chapter applies to you! Even if you are not going the full "creating an innovation environment" route, the issues addressed in this chapter can trip you up if you're not careful. Read on!

> **Top 8 Innovation Killers**
>
> ☠ Not aligning projects with the company's strategy
>
> ☠ Not getting buy-in and ownership from the CEO, executive team, and department managers
>
> ☠ Not having a simple, but effective structure that is used by everyone
>
> ☠ Not allocating resources to all parts of your innovation environment efforts
>
> ☠ Not developing clear goals and measurements in advance
>
> ☠ Not creating a long-term innovation culture
>
> ☠ Not training and coaching everyone on innovation
>
> ☠ Not having a system for collecting ideas

THE VALUE OF TESTING

Test your idea before you fully implement it (although this may not always be possible depending on what you are doing):

- If it's a product, create a prototype, and have a couple of customers try it out.

- If it's a service, outline the concept, and then try it out on a customer you know well.

- If it's a change to a process, it's ideal to test it by running the new process alongside the old process (this is called parallel testing). This way, if something bad happens with the new process, the old process is still working, and you haven't created havoc.

If this is not possible, then you want to make sure you simulate the new process by walking through every step of it to see where something might go wrong.

Testing can cost money, especially if you need to bring in outside experts to help you set up your testing methodology. For example, your optimum testing methodology may use prototyping and consumer feedback, neither of which you have the in-house expertise to manage.

Get Some Testing Help

Don't underestimate the importance of testing. It's much easier to fix things in this stage than after you fully roll out your innovation. To learn more about testing, I recommend either of the project management books I have listed in Appendix B. Also, the *Innovator's Toolkit*[7] talks about some different testing methodologies. If you need outside experts, they can range from those who have been involved with a similar project to certified experts in a specific type of testing.

helpfulhints

ADJUST ON THE FLY

It's not uncommon during an innovation project for the project leader and project team to get married to the original idea and those steps necessary to implement it. More often than not, as you put the many smart minds of your project team to work, additional thoughts and ideas may surface that could be a major improvement to the original concept. The CIO, executive sponsor, and project leader should be looking out for these opportunities and be willing to stop, regroup, adjust, and get rolling again. Don't confuse this concept with the next section.

FEATURE CREEP? DON'T LET IT HAPPEN!

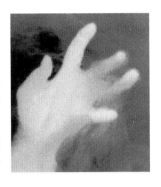

Feature creep is different from adjusting on the fly, but sometimes it's hard to distinguish between the two. Once again, as you travel down the road to put your idea into action, your project team or people it works with outside of the team will have many ideas to make the end product or process even better. It is the project leader's difficult task to discern between the "nice to have" feature creep ideas and the "we have to make this change" because it's a big kind of improvement. The best thing you can do with the feature creep items is to put them on a list for future versions of the idea you are rolling out.

ACCOUNTABILITY

This topic was covered in the structure chapter, but it is such an important concept that it needs to be discussed here. One of the key duties for your project manager is to make sure every step has a person assigned to it and a due date associated with it. In a perfect world, no team member will ever miss a deadline. Also in a perfect world, a team member will let the project manager know that they will not meet the deadline and it will be revised. If a due date passes with no proactive adjustment by the team member, the project manager has to point out the missed deadline in the weekly meeting and get the negligent team member to commit to a new deadline. If it continues to happen, the project leader, department head for that team member, and CIO may need to get involved. I don't want to sound mean; you can be very empathetic and very firm at the same time. Staying on top of this will ensure that your project doesn't lose its momentum.

OVERCOMMUNICATE!

It's tempting to copy and paste the Chapter 6 section about culture and communication here because it's so important. Instead, it will suffice to tell you that, as busy as you are, you must make sure you make time to talk to your team sponsor and team members on a regular basis, and to communicate to the executive team about the innovation's progress and risks. As was mentioned in *Bottom-Up Innovation*, communicating about the risks is important because it isn't worth losing your job due to a bad surprise. Even if you are an executive, that could happen. You are taking a risk. That's why communication, including stressing the risk of failure and constantly updating about the project's status, is so important.

TEAM DYNAMICS

Attitude Is Everything

When a group of people works closely together for a long period of time, chances are there will be issues. I've seen withholding of information, belittling, meeting piracy, obstinacy, and even yelling. Don't let these things slide. Remember, everything (good and bad) flows downhill. The project leader must:

- ➢ Keep a positive, "we shall overcome" attitude.
- ➢ Nip any of the negative signs listed above in the butt immediately.
- ➢ Make the meetings fun: Mix it up; bring dessert; have a potluck; change the venue.
- ➢ Recognize someone at least once each meeting.
- ➢ Keep the meetings on track; follow the rules (don't waste meeting time by letting everyone say what they are working on; the team should know that from the project plan steps sheet).

It is the project leader's responsibility to watch for team dysfunction, which can occur at the outset of the project or creep in through a side door sometime during the life of a project. Patrick Lencioni's engaging book *The Five Dysfuctions of a Team*[21] has a great list of five dysfunctions to watch out for:

➢ Absence of trust
➢ Fear of conflict
➢ Lack of commitment
➢ Avoidance of accountability
➢ Inattention to results

Lencioni identifies trust as the biggest culprit, which I agree with and discuss in Chapter 6. In his book, he includes a team assessment for identifying dysfunctions, as well as tips for how to overcome some of the issues listed above.

Diversity Is King!

Aside from discussions elsewhere in this book that indicate the best team is made up of both adaptors and innovators, other kinds of diversity are as important for creating that "perfect team." The book *Managing Creativity and Innovation*[22] talks about the perfect team having contrasting characteristics such as beginners and experience; freedom and discipline; play and professionalism; and improvisation and planning. This is true not only for your project teams, but also for your brainstorming groups and evaluation teams.

BREAKING DOWN SILOS

Many times, you will need team members from a number of other departments within your company. Some of those department heads may be anti-innovation, or they may be very controlling, or they may not be willing to give up any of their valuable resources, or they may be the "if it's not my idea, I want no part in it" type of people.

This can be a real tough issue. The best way to handle this is to do a bit of coddling by taking them out to lunch, and talking about how important they and their department's involvement are in the project. Talk about how the success of the project will bestow accolades on anyone involved. Tell them that, even though they will not be on the team, you would like to be able to seek their advice as you move through the project. If none of this works, you tried. It's time to pull out the power card: Have the CIO, executive sponsor, or even the president talk to them, and mandate their contribution of resources.

Simply Innovate

This happens to be the name of my company, but an important point for you to think about in all your efforts is to keep it simple. Tom Kelley writes in *The Art of Innovation*:[12] "Make your product or service work faster and simpler, and it will probably succeed." Kelley uses the one-click ordering process pioneered by Amazon (which I love) as an example. Obviously, I live by this concept; so should you.

helpfulhints

Chapter 9: Final Confessions. Tell Me Your Story!

We've covered a lot of ground in a relatively few number of pages. My goal is to keep innovation simple enough for you to get your arms around it, but to give you enough details so that you are not missing any big concepts. The other goal is to make innovation actionable, not theoretical. How did I do?

This book is an innovation in and of itself. Therefore, I want to learn how this book impacted you so I can improve upon future revisions. I can't do this without your honest feedback. I appreciate all your comments. If you had a great success, let me know, and I may use your story (with your permission) in my book or on my website. Please go to www.simplyinnovate.net and use the comments section. You can also email me at feedback@simplyinnovate.net.

Do you enjoy innovating? If so, you can do the following:

☞ Read *Bottom-Up Innovation*. Hopefully you've done that already since, as an executive, you need to know the whole innovation picture (and the fact that you already own it helps, too).
☞ Keep learning more about innovation. See Appendix B for some books I recommend. There are great blogs and other resources that focus on specific areas of innovation. Go to the Helpful Resources tab at www.simplyinnovate.net for links to some of these resources.
☞ Start with one small incremental simple innovation, but use the process in this book to do it.
☞ Keep influencing people around you. Look for those opportunities to influence; they will come up.

Part III Action Summary

Chapter 8

> ➢ Make sure each project includes some testing methodology, if at all possible.
> ➢ Educate and monitor the project to ensure that the sections in this chapter are being followed (i.e., adjust, no feature creep, accountability).
> ➢ Overcommunicate! Double check your communication plan.
> ➢ Make sure team dynamics are addressed in your education plan.
> ➢ Keep an eye out for silos, and make sure the appropriate people help tear them down.

Chapter 9

> ➢ Send me feedback about how to improve this book and any success stories at www.simplyinnovate.net.

Top-Down Innovation: Websites and Credits

Website References

❖ Chapter 2 – How to Boost your Creativity – 20 ways to increase your creativity: -
http://psychology.about.com/od/cognitivepsychology/tp/how-to-boost-creativity.htm

❖ Chapter 2 – How to Boost your Creativity – 20 ways to increase your creativity:

❖ http://creativethinking.net/WP01_Home.htm

❖ Chapter 5 – Kill the Starving Monkeys – Watch out for the "too many projects" syndrome:
http://www.informationweek.com/news/208403794

❖ Chapter 6 – People and Culture – Idea software and idea consulting companies that put on great seminars and conferences: www.spigit.com and www.bmgi.com

❖ Chapter 6 – Why I Hire People Who Fail – How to move your company from good to great:
http://blogs.hbr.org/cs/2011/12/why_i_hire_people_who_fail.html

❖ Chapter 6 – Time and Its Impact on Culture – Corel's Virtual Garage program:
http://www.ideachampions.com/weblogs/archives/2007/08/its_innovation.shtml

❖ Chapter 7 – Get Out of the Office – Patrick Lefler's blog on getting out: http://www.innovationexcellence.com/blog/2011/05/22/get-out-of-the-office-and-talk-to-customers

❖ Chapter 7 – How to Collect Ideas – Adobe's idea site:
http://na5.brightidea.com/ct/s.bix?c=8FBBEA8F-D8E6-4E34-A7C1-7C74FB3B4EFA

❖ Chapter 7 – How to Collect Ideas – GE's idea site:
http://challenge.ecomagination.com/ideas

❖ Chapter 7 – How to Encourage Ideas – Article on gamification:
http://www.gamasutra.com/view/news/34111/Analyst_Over_Half_Of_Innovation_Companies_To_Adopt_Gamification_By_2015.php

Credits

1. Cracking the Code of Effective Communication: Organization Size and Style Is Driving Innovation Success. Future Think LLC, June 2007: http://www.scribd.com/doc/7671082/Cracking-the-Code-of-Effective-Innovation

2. Lockheed Martin's Skunk Works: http://www.lockheedmartin.com/us/aeronautics/skunkworks.html

3. P&G's Innovation Labs: https://secure3.verticali.net/pg-connection-portal/ctx/noauth/SubmitInnovation.do

4. Coca-Cola's Innovation Lab: http://www.thecoca-colacompany.com/ourcompany/innovation.html

5. Barry, Katie, Ellen Domb, and Michael S. Slocum. TRIZ — What Is TRIZ? *The TRIZ Journal*: http://www.triz-journal.com/archives/what_is_triz

6. Six Sigma Online: http://www.sixsigmaonline.org/index.html

7. CSR Globe. General Motor's Corp: http://www.csrglobe.com/login/companies/generalmotors.html

8. The Coca-Cola Company. Mission, Vision, & Values: http://www.thecoca-colacompany.com/ourcompany/mission_vision_values.html

9. Silverstein, David, Philip Samuel, and Neil DeCarlo. *The Innovator's Toolkit: 50+ Techniques for Predictable and Sustainable Organic Growth*. John Wiley & Sons Inc., 2009: http://www.innovatorstoolkit.com

10. Dr. Michael Kirton's Adaption-Innovation theory: http://www.kaicentre.com

11. The Myers & Briggs Foundation: http://www.myersbriggs.org

12. Collins, Jim. *Good to Great: Why Some Companies Make the Leap … and Others Don't*. HarperCollins, 2011: http://www.jimcollins.com/books

13. Stibel, Jeff. *Why I Hire People Who Fail*. Harvard Business Review Blog Network, Dec. 9, 2011: http://blogs.hbr.org/cs/2011/12/why_i_hire_people_who_fail.html

14. Kelley, Tom. *The Art of Innovation*. IDEO, 2003: http://theartofinnovation.com/default.htm

15. Wikipedia. Google Employee's Innovation Time Off:
http://en.wikipedia.org/wiki/Google

16. 3M Corp. A Century of Innovation: The 3M Story:
http://multimedia.3m.com/mws/mediawebserver?77777Xxam
fIVO&Wwo_Pw5_W7HYxTHfxajYv7HYv7H777777--

17. Boynton, Andy, and Bill Fischer. Selling the Best Hour of the
Day to Yourself. ChiefExecutive.net, Mar. 3, 2011:
http://chiefexecutive.net/selling-the-best-hour-of-the-day-to-
yourself

18. McGirt, Ellen. Innovation Wednesday: Corel's Virtual Garage.
Fast Company, Aug. 22, 2007:
http://www.fastcompany.com/blog/ellen-mcgirt/innovation-
wednesday/innovation-wednesday-corels-virtual-garage

19. Atlassian's Fed-Ex Day:
http://confluence.atlassian.com/display/DEV/Atlassian+FedE
x+Days

20. Lefler, Patrick. *Get Out of the Office and Talk to Customers.*
Innovation Excellence Blog, May 22, 2011:
http://www.innovationexcellence.com/blog/2011/05/22/get-
out-of-the-office-and-talk-to-customers

21. Lencioni, Patrick M. *The Five Dysfuctions of a Team: A Leadership
Fable.* Jossey-Bass, 2002:
http://www.josseybass.com/WileyCDA/WileyTitle/productC
d-0787960756,descCd-reviews.html

22. Harvard Business School Press. *Managing Creativity and
Innovation.* Harvard Business Press Books, 2003:
http://hbr.org/product/harvard-business-essentials-guide-to-
managing-crea/an/1121-PBK-ENG

Photo Credits

1. Chapter 1 – Street signs courtesy of Hampton Roads Partnership at http://www.flickr.com/photos/hamptonroadspartnership/535 1622717/sizes/z/in/photostream/
2. Chapter 1 – Old School image courtesy of Adam Pieniazek at http://www.flickr.com/photos/adampieniazek/2784992613/si zes/l/in/photostream/
3. Times square image courtesy of Matt Blasi Design & Photography at http://www.flickr.com/photos/mattblasidesigns/404331 3584/sizes/o/in/photostream/
4. Chapter 2 – Home construction courtesy of Concrete Forms at http://www.flickr.com/photos/concrete_forms/5237652 08/sizes/z/in/photostream/
5. Chapter 6 – Child image by greyshine at http://www.flickr.com/photos/greyshine/5853298005/s izes/z/in/photostream/
6. Chapter 6 – Woman behind transparent paper courtesy of I Woke Up Today at http://www.flickr.com/photos/22036287@N06/4626239826/si zes/l/in/photostream/
7. Chapter 6 - Stop Motion People Creating courtesy of VFS Digital Design http://www.flickr.com/photos/vfsdigitaldesign/6590322 397/
8. Balls courtesy of Dennis Errgang at http://www.flickr.com/photos/baccharus/5619400287/
9. Creepy Hand courtesy of Keoni Cabral at http://www.flickr.com/photos/keoni101/5134539639/
10. Silos courtesy of Doc Searls at http://www.flickr.com/photos/docsearls/5500714140/

IDENTIFY YOUR BUSINESS CHALLENGE FORMS

BOTTOM-UP INNOVATION – CHAPTER 4

Use these forms to fill in your discussions with people during your efforts to make sure you've identified the right business challenge. Be sure to list the name of whom you talked to and any significant takeaways.

Date   Spoke With

Notes: _____

_____

_____

Date   Spoke With

Notes: _____

_____

_____

Date   Spoke With

Notes: _____

_____

Date   Spoke With

☐☐/☐☐ _____

Notes: _____

_____

_____

Date   Spoke With

☐☐/☐☐ _____

Notes: _____

_____

_____

Date   Spoke With

☐☐/☐☐ _____

Notes: _____

_____

_____

IDEAS

BOTTOM-UP INNOVATION – CHAPTER 5

Log your ideas on these pages. Use additional paper if you have more than 14 ideas. Be sure each idea has a unique number; you will refer to them this way in the next step.

5)

6)

7)

8)

9)

10 〉

11 〉

12 〉

13 〉

14 〉

ADVANCED FILTERING FORM

	Idea					TOTAL
1						
2						
3						
4						
5						
6						
7						
8						
9						
10						
11						
12						
13						

Major and Minor Steps

List the major steps below. Once you write them down, number them in the order you will complete them (some things can't be done before others). Don't worry if you have to come back and revise this. Start by writing down the No. 1 major step from the previous page; then underneath it, list all the minor steps that need to be completed first. Do this for all the major steps. You may need a couple of pages for this.

ID #	Done	% Done	Task Name	Duration	Start	Finish	Name
1		10%	Consignment Project	101 days	2/2/2011	6/2/2011	
2	✓	100%	Project Manager introduction call	1 day	3/25/2011	3/25/2011	Maggie
3	✓	100%	Project ROI and Charter	12 days	2/2/2011	2/17/2011	Mark
4		20%	**Identify the Participating Retail Locations**	47 days	2/2/2011	4/7/2011	Frank
5	✓	100%	Print listing of existing stores	12 days	2/2/2011	2/17/2011	Frank
6		0%	Delete any that have lack of space	45 days	2/2/2011	4/3/2011	Frank
7		0%	Submit list to real estate dept for approval	2 days	2/2/2011	4/7/2011	Frank
8		24%	**Legal/Risk Analysis**	28 days	2/2/2011	3/25/2011	Stephanie
9	✓	100%	Create draft consignment agreement	12 days	2/2/2011	2/17/2011	Stephanie
10		20%	Review insurance requirements	28 days	2/28/2011	3/25/2011	Stephanie
11		0%	Get required sign-offs	12 days	2/17/2011	2/28/2011	Stephanie
12		0%	**Marketing of Program and PR**	32 days	3/26/2011	5/8/2011	Jeanette
13		0%	Outreach to existing partners	22 days	3/26/2011	4/24/2011	Jeanette
14		0%	Placement of information sheet	22 days	3/26/2011	4/24/2011	Jeanette
15		0%	Markeing brochure for existing customer base	32 days	3/26/2011	5/8/2011	Jeanette
16		0%	Website information and updates	32 days	3/26/2011	5/8/2011	Jeanette
17		0%	Present PR ideas	22 days	3/26/2011	4/24/2011	Jeanette

APPENDIX B
RECOMMENDED BOOKS

There are a lot of innovation books, some of which cover in depth only a certain aspect of innovation, and others that cover multiple subjects. There also are a couple of good project management books and some books that are not specifically about innovation, which are great business books that will make you think. This list is not meant to be comprehensive; it is merely a list of books I think you will find useful.

Books are listed by category.

Science and Theory of Ideas, Innovation, and Success

What Customers Want: Using Outcome-Driven Innovation to Create Breakthrough Products and Services (McGraw-Hill; 2005) by Anthony W. Ulwick. This book uses the term "outcome-driven" innovation, which is a scientific approach to new product and service creation. The author spends most of the book describing how individuals should focus on the "metrics that customers use to measure success when executing the jobs, tasks, or activities they are trying to get done" to come up with ideas. He writes one chapter on prioritizing projects, but it is discussed at a high level.

Creating an Innovation Environment

Strategic Innovation (Jossey-Bass; 2003) by Nancy Tennant Snyder and Deborah L. Duarte. Read how Whirlpool successfully embedded innovation into every corner of its company. This book includes some great insights and learnings from their experiences.

Market and Growth Strategies

The Innovator's Solution: Creating and Sustaining Successful Growth (Harvard Business Press; 2003) by Clayton M. Christensen and Michael E. Raynor. This book focuses on companies expanding by being "disruptors," a term used for a product that is a radical change from what previously existed. People looking for quick fixes may find the charts, diagrams, and extensive footnotes daunting. It is geared toward large companies and stays pretty theoretical most of the time. I like the concept of sustaining vs. disruptive innovation.

Idea Creation

The Art of Innovation: Lessons in Creativity from IDEO, America's Leading Design Firm (Broadway Business; 2001) by Tom Kelley, Jonathan Littman, and Tom Peters. This book really teaches indirectly by telling great stories. It talks about how observing regular people at work and play is key to coming up with a new product or solution. It focuses on IDEO's teams and inventions.

Borrowing Brilliance: The Six Steps to Business Innovation by Building on the Ideas of Others (Gotham Books; 2009) by David Kord Murray. This book focuses on the concept that the key to the creative process is borrowing ideas from others. It is strong on the first phase of innovation: coming up with ideas. It also discusses some of the other phases of innovation.

Thinkertoys: A Handbook of Creative-Thinking Techniques (Ten Speed Press; 2006) by Michael Michalko. *Thinkertoys* has 30 techniques that train you how to generate new ideas. Some of the techniques are pretty good; others are a bit weird. This and *The Innovator's Toolkit* (see below) are two books I might refer to people who want to find more techniques on innovation.

Innovation Structure

The Game Changer: How to Drive Revenue and Profit Growth Thru Innovation (Crown Business; 2008) by A. G. Lafley and Ram Charan. The author was the CEO of P&G, so most of the book describes P&G's innovation efforts and successes. It probably comes the closest to talking someone all the way through the innovation process, but it doesn't talk much about project management.

Innovation Tools

The Innovator's Toolkit: 50+ Techniques for Predictable and Sustainable Organic Growth (Wiley; 2008) by David Silverstein, Philip Samuel, and Neil DeCarlo. The cool thing about this book is it gives you tools for what the authors describe as the four phases of innovation: define, discover, develop, and demonstrate. Some of these tools are easy, but many require very sophisticated knowledge. This book gives you a big pile of tools that you can use — some easy and some that require experts.

Open Innovation

The Innovation Killer: How What We Know Limits What We Can Imagine — and What Smart Companies Are Doing About It (AMACOM; 2006) by Cynthia Barton Rabe. This entire book focuses on open innovation — where you use outsiders to stimulate innovation. This is a very important concept, especially for small businesses.

Innovation Management

Managing Creativity and Innovation (Harvard Business Press; 2003) by Harvard Business School Press. A relatively concise book at 130 pages (plus appendices), this book does a good job explaining idea creation. It also discusses filtering ideas, although this concept is not as clean and easy to understand as it is in my book.

General Innovation

The Innovator's Guide to Growth (Harvard Business Press; 2008) by Scott D. Anthony, Mark W. Johnson, Joseph V. Sinfield, and Elizabeth J. Altman. This book is a very good complement to *Top-Down and Bottom-Up Innovation* as it delves deeply into how to identify opportunities, and it discusses the concept of disruptive innovation in depth. It also discusses emergent strategies and has a good chapter on innovation metrics.

Project Management

5-Phase Project Management: A Practical Planning and Implementation Guide (Addison-Wesley Publishing; 1992) by Joseph Weiss and Robert Wysocki. At 110 pages, this is one of the older but still one of the best books on project management. Many books written since use a lot of the principles in this book, but spend twice as many pages on the subject. This book does not talk about creativity, ideas, or filtering of ideas. It also assumes that you have experienced dedicated project managers, which many companies do not have.

Project Management for Dummies (Wiley Publishing; 2007) by Stanley E. Portny. This book delves very deeply into project management if you need this knowledge. It does explain some very technical things as simply as possible.

Other Books

Blue Ocean Strategy (Harvard Business School Publishing Corp.; 2005) by W. Chan Kim and Renee Mauborgne. The authors argue that tomorrow's leading companies will succeed not by battling competitors, but by creating "blue oceans" of uncontested market space ripe for growth.

Made to Stick (Random House Publishing Group; 2008) by Chip Heath and Dan Heath. In this book, the authors tell you why some ideas survive and others die. They reveal the anatomy of ideas that stick, and they explain ways to make ideas stickier.

Good to Great (Harper Business; 2001) by Jim Collins. Even though some of the companies mentioned in this book as "great" have fallen on hard times, there are so many great principles in this book that I believe can help you in your company, that it is well worth reading.

Made in the USA
Charleston, SC
20 April 2012